"Tav Spar[illegible] hesis of psychology, spirituality, an[illegible] ugh his wisdom, depth of knowledge and heart, Tav helps us to rediscover the Twelve Steps at a new and deeper level. The Wide Open Door *masterfully bridges the gap between the field of addictions and psychology which has left many clinicians and recovering people ill at ease.* The Wide Open Door *is an important contribution to the addictions field."*

—Rokelle Lerner
International lecturer, trainer, consultant, and
author of *Daily Affirmations for Adult Children of Alcoholics* and
Affirmations for the Inner Child.

"Tav Sparks has provided a significant service in illuminating the way that deep Twelve Step recovery practice aligns with both ancient and contemporary ways of spiritual transformation."

—Linda Leonard, Ph.D.
Author of *Witness to the Fire: Creativity and the Veil of Addiction*

"In The Wide Open Door, *Tav Sparks skillfully weaves the wisdom of the Twelve Steps with insights from spiritual systems and transpersonal psychology. This articulate, compassionate guide to recovery and personal growth is a valuable tool, pointing to new directions in the understanding and treatment of addictions."*

—Christina Grof
Author of *The Thirst for Wholeness: Attachment, Addiction, and the Spiritual Path*

"A *valuable resource for anyone seeking a better understanding of the healing process and the relationship of psychology and spirituality to health and well being."*

—Frances Vaughan, Ph.D.
Author of *The Inward Arc*

"A *groundbreaking book . . . By drawing on the empirical wisdom of the Twelve Step traditions and the theory and practice of transpersonal psychology,* The Wide Open Door *offers exciting new perspectives in the addictions field."*

—Stanislav Grof, M.D.
Author of *The Holotropic Mind* and *The Adventure of Self-Discovery*

THE WIDE OPEN DOOR

About the author

Tav Sparks is a writer and therapist living in Mill Valley, California. Since 1985, he has led numerous workshops throughout the United States and Canada in transpersonal approaches to wellness and recovery. Formerly an addictions therapist, he has been an original theorist in the emerging field of transpersonal addiction and codependence recovery. He has also presented practical models for implementing this approach in treatment settings.

To contact Tav Sparks or receive workshop information, please write to:

Tav Sparks
38 Miller Avenue, Suite 158
Mill Valley, CA 94941

THE WIDE OPEN DOOR

The Twelve Steps, Spiritual Tradition, And the New Psychology

Tav Sparks

Hazelden Educational Materials
Center City, Minnesota 55012-0176

5 4 3 2 1 97 96 95 94 93

ISBN: 0-89486-867-5

Editor's note

Hazelden Educational Materials offers a variety of information on chemical dependency and related areas. Our publications do not necessarily represent Hazelden's programs, nor do they officially speak for any Twelve Step organization.

The Twelve Steps are reprinted with permission of Alcoholics Anonymous World Services, Inc. Permission to reprint the Twelve Steps does not mean that Alcoholics Anonymous has reviewed or approved the contents of this publication, nor that AA agrees with the views expressed herein. The views expressed herein are solely those of the author. AA is a program of recovery from alcoholism. Use of the Twelve Steps in connection with programs and activities that are patterned after AA, but that address other problems, does not imply otherwise.

The stories in this book are real. In all cases, names have been changed to protect the anonymity of the people involved.

Contents

Acknowledgments

My experience, strength, and hope are intimately interwoven with that of many people who have been instrumental, directly or indirectly, in the writing of this book. It is not possible to acknowledge them all by name. However, some are so important that they deserve to be mentioned.

I wish to thank first my family—my father, Gus; my mother, Patty; my two sisters, Trisha and Jackie; my brother, Bill; and my brother-in-law, John—for their love and for enduring my adventure. I am grateful for all my friends in Macon, Georgia, and especially the Charter Lake team who gave me a chance: Bill, Al, Roy, Jim, Gail, and all the rest. Thanks also to Jacquie and Greg for our journey together.

I will never forget Frank and Les. And thanks to Charlie and David for all their guidance.

It is difficult to express the depth of my feelings for Christina and Stan—for their guidance, support, and friendship. And I hold a special place in my heart for Stan, whose work has been my greatest inspiration.

To Hazelden, but especially to Judy, I am forever indebted. Thank you for believing in this project. And I am grateful for everyone who has traveled the Broad Highway before me, and for all those with whom I am traveling now, for showing me the way.

I save a special acknowledgment for my wonderful sons, Ason and Bryn, who are my truest teachers. Finally, I wish to thank Cary, my wife, constant companion, best friend, and wise and loving critic, without whom my life could not possibly be so blessed.

Introduction—At Another Turning Point

We are deeply aware that we stand upon the threshold of a great door which opens wide into our future.

—Bill W.

My poor heart's humble door is standing open wide / Be gracious, Lord, and enter there but once and quench its thirst!

—Ramakrishna

We in recovery are no strangers to change. We are well aware of the importance of what Carl Jung called a radical "rearrangement" of consciousness. Nor is it farfetched to compare our own transformation in recovery with the dramatic upheavals that we see taking place daily on the world stage. Recovery, as well as modern planetary evolution, requires that we continually surrender our ideas about the way things are and be open to whatever our Higher Power may bring us.

Yet many feel that in terms of both individual and global evolution, the current wave of change is much more dramatic than it has ever been before. The radical shifts that are now occurring are no less than quantum leaps. They are so profound that many are finding themselves without their traditional psychological and spiritual groundings. Even our worldviews, the very bases of how we think, do not seem as solid as they once were.

At times like these, we may tend to hold on and to resist change even more. The result of this resistance on a collective level is some form of revolution. On a personal level, it is an increasing sense of restlessness and disease that often culminates in a deep psychological and spiritual crisis. For us on the Twelve Step path, these crises can be characterized by the question, Is this all there is? They bear so little resemblance to what has gone before them that they essentially demand of us what author Ralph Blum has called an "empty-handed leap into the void." At this point, our entire way of thinking and even our sobriety are up for grabs.

Fortunately, over the past few decades, a worldview that combines a new science, philosophy, and psychology has developed, providing a way for us to make these latest transitions. Moreover, this new perspective seems to be validated by the great spiritual traditions of the world. Yet, even though the purpose of the Twelve Steps is psychological and spiritual change, thus far there has been no language and structure to make this vision of change a practical reality for us in recovery. The question many are asking themselves now is, Can the Twelve Steps take us all the way through these quantum leaps?

I first became aware of the power of radical psychological and spiritual upheaval in the late 1960s through psychedelic exploration. During this cycle of great turmoil, the Higher Power became a reality for me for the first time in my life. I had many experiences that convinced me of my connection to humanity and the universe at large. In addition, I sensed I was part of a global revolution in attitudes and consciousness itself that now seems, these many years later, to be felt worldwide. I also spent a good deal of time during that era studying world psychological and spiritual texts that helped to validate many of the experiences I was having.

The connectedness I enjoyed in the sixties was followed in the seventies by the pain of my addiction and a sense of absolute separation. How quickly addiction makes a mockery of spiritual principles! If the sixties were in some way a heaven, then the seventies were definitely a hell. And for me, hell was a state of total aloneness—absolute separation from myself, others, and a Higher Power. Perhaps my greatest shame was in being consumed by obsession and compulsion, while knowing in the depths of my being that there was another way to live.

I spent most of the seventies in the streets and in the woods, doing everything I could to stay high. Every few years I wound up on a mental ward with delirium tremens, wasted body, and broken spirit. And through it all, I left behind me a wake of confused friends and hurt family. I was in and out of recovery meetings much of that time, fighting the inexorable truth that I would one day have to get clean and sober, or die.

In 1979 I underwent what I call my "wasteland experience." This was a profound surrender, my First Step experience that brought me irrevocably into the world of the Twelve Steps and recovery. All the slogans and principles I had heard "with my mind" during the seventies suddenly made perfect sense. I knew I was home at last.

I spent the first part of the eighties learning how to live on planet Earth. I already knew how to fly. But I knew next to nothing about how to be a human being with normal everyday responsibilities and relationships. Modern teacher Ram Dass says that it is okay to get "out there." But we should not become so spiritual that we forget our zip code. For me, I did not even have a zip code I could forget. I had to learn how to comb my hair, brush my teeth, write a check, and be at work on time. I had to *get* a zip code! This is what being spiritual meant for me in those days.

Becoming an addictions therapist after a few years in recovery seemed to be a response to the awakening of some of the old feelings of connectedness that I recalled from my sixties exploration. The necessity of service appears to go hand in hand with connectedness. And the program showed me in no uncertain terms the importance of carrying the message. So it was with great excitement and hope, as well as a sense of naivete, that I went to work as a therapist in a treatment facility.

I will never forget my days as a rookie counselor. Our staff was dedicated to the principles of psychological and spiritual recovery as they were presented in the Big Book* and supported by the best the treatment field had to offer at that time. Our goal was to

---

*Alcoholics Anonymous, 3d ed. (New York: A.A. World Services, Inc., 1976).

provide an atmosphere where seekers could experience the First Step. And we did well. We knew that the key to recovery was spirituality. However, I soon learned that even though treatment is based on the philosophy that spirituality is essential, its principal methods to bring about this spiritual awakening have been for the most part *psychological*. Although the field seems to have a great deal of psychological expertise, it does not have at its disposal equally effective methods to make spirituality a *reality* for seekers.

It was with the loss of some of my naivete and hope that I tried to accept the limitations of treatment. Yet, I still felt we could do more. It was not that our center was unique in this regard. It seemed to me that there was a general malaise in the treatment field altogether. Even those centers which were using powerful techniques still did not have a comprehensive framework that could support deep spiritual experiences. Moreover, mental health also appeared to be caught in the same narrow psychological perspective and thus could not avail itself of spiritual approaches.

At this same time I was also undergoing a crisis in my own recovery. I had long since fallen off my pink cloud and had settled in for the recovery journey, one day at a time. I knew that a Higher Power was the key to my growth. But somehow I felt that there were blocks in my being where the energy of this Higher Power had not yet penetrated. I went to therapy and began to work on my family-of-origin and codependence issues. But I *still* felt a sense of dis-ease. Even though I knew that my Higher Power was healing me, there just did not seem to be a way to bring this Power to bear on those areas where I felt blocked.

Simultaneously with my own personal unrest went a professional dilemma as well. If I myself did not know how to make fully conscious the deeper layers of my being of which I was gradually becoming aware, then how could I be an effective guide for the other seekers in my group? In 1984, at this point of personal and professional crisis, I had the opportunity to undergo a powerful Eleventh Step method, which resulted in a spiritual experience. My conscious contact with my Higher Power greatly improved. The episode also deepened my experience of surrender, and generally enriched my practice of all the Steps.

I realized that a great circle of my being had somehow completed itself. One half of the circle had been my sixties insights and experiences, where I had first made contact with a Higher Power, humanity, and the universe at large. I understood that my psychedelic exploration was not just a part of my addiction, but was, in fact, a legitimate attempt to answer the most profound call of my being—to move toward wholeness. The second half of the circle was my Twelve Step recovery and my absolute commitment to answer the same call moving me toward my Higher Power, *drug-free*, one day at a time.

Through the use of this Eleventh Step method, the two halves of the circle came together in a wonderful completion for me. From that point on, I could reach back and welcome what my Higher Power had given me in the sixties. I could do this *at the same time* that I currently followed my Twelve Step path. Now I knew that there were powerful *nondrug* methods to support Twelve Step recovery. These Eleventh Step techniques would at the same time deepen recovery to include the spiritual search as it has been envisioned by seekers worldwide for millennia.

To validate and support my inner work, I once again explored the way world cultures described the spiritual journey. I found that in addition to consciousness research, there was also a new force in Western psychology that included spirituality. This movement was known as *transpersonal psychology*. This discovery was particularly exciting for me, because I could envision its being the perfect helpmate for the Twelve Steps in a new and effective recovery perspective.

I studied the philosophical foundations of the Twelve Step movement and discovered that recovery was already deeply rooted in psychology and spirituality. Bill W.'s own consciousness research as presented in *Pass It On* provided a wonderful validation of my own sixties experiences. It helped me to see that I was on the right track and that I did not have to reject that important phase of my exploration.

I soon realized that the dilemma I had recently undergone was just a personal example of a collective crisis that was affecting people all over the world. New findings in physics and other sciences, coupled with insights from spiritual exploration and consciousness research, are requiring that we begin to see ourselves, and the nature of reality itself, in new ways. These changes seem to be a part of the gradual evolution of world culture and philosophy toward some future wholeness. But because they are so radical, they are contributing to all sorts of crises in the lives of individuals, as well as in societies at large.

Many of us have begun to envision how these great upheavals are similar to what happens to addicts and codependents during the First Step crisis, just before the surrender experience. Every facet of planetary life—from the environment, to the economy, to the restructuring of national boundaries—seems to be in turmoil in much the same way as addicts when they enter recovery. Parallel with these world changes, seekers everywhere, in all stages of Twelve Step practice, are reporting that they are going through a profound yet confusing stage of their recovery journey. For some, it is marked by the question, Is this all there is? Others feel that they are at a crossroads, where they are actually wondering if recovery can continue to work for them. Still others sense that they are doing exactly what their Higher Power has led them to do, but they are unable to find any support for their new insights.

There is already a body of knowledge that characterizes the traditional recovery field. There is also a substantial base of theory that supports the latest findings related to the transpersonal perspective in science, psychology, and spirituality. But there is so far no work that bridges traditional recovery and the transpersonal perspective. There is nothing that introduces one to the other, or translates the language of each into the metaphor of the other, so that both become understandable to seekers interested in their synergistic possibilities.

It has long been my belief that these new observations in science, psychology, and spirituality are the pathways to enlarging our understanding of the true power and depth of Twelve Step practice. But thus far there has been no framework—no language, method, and structure—to bring these disciplines together. Therefore, toward that end, I have written *The Wide Open Door.* First and foremost, it is an effort to validate and support those recovery seekers who feel that there really may be "something more" for them than what they have previously discovered about recovery. I have tried to write it in such a way that those seekers unfamiliar with this new perspective will be able to relate to it without much difficulty.

This work is the result not only of my own experience, strength, and hope, but also that of many others with whom I have had the opportunity to share and work since 1984. I have tried to present it not as *the truth*, but as *one way* to consider the Twelve Step adventure. I myself have had many of the experiences I describe as being possible for those on the journey of deep recovery; these are my "experiences and strengths."

Those places where I describe the far horizons of the Steps, the Promises, and the recovery movement itself fall under the category of my "hopes." I *hope* that these horizons can be reached by all of us. And I also hope that this synthesis can be of service to others who may find themselves at a crossroads in their recovery and who are considering exploring the deeper mysteries of the Steps. If nothing else, *The Wide Open Door* can be what Joseph Campbell referred to as a "call to adventure" for each of us to find our own way on what Bill W. called the Broad Highway. Ultimately, it is an opportunity for me to express my gratitude for my own recovery, and to give back just a little of the great gift that has been so freely given to me.

CHAPTER ONE

At the Crossroads—
Is This All There Is?

> *How could there be human means to cure what the divine fire has made sick?*
>
> —Teresa of Avila

> *More than most people, I think, alcoholics want to know who they are, what this life is about, whether they have a divine origin or an appointed destiny, and whether there is a system of cosmic justice and love.*
>
> —Bill W.

Since this book is about rediscovering the Twelve Steps at a new and deeper level, its ultimate message is an exciting and joyful one. Yet we are familiar with how it feels to be at a midway point, where we are frequently faced with some difficult choices on our journey. Often, this place can feel very different from the Promises we hope will come true for us somewhere down the road. So, remembering that before surrender there is usually a struggle, we will deal in this first chapter with some of the dark hours we may experience before the dawn reveals our new road into the deeper mystery of the Steps.

EARLY DAYS

If we are in touch with the core of our program, it is easy to remember our struggle with obsession and compulsion. But can we remember when the obsession and compulsion lifted? Most of us have many fond memories of that special time to go along with the nightmare remembrances of the shakes, sleepless nights, and "one hundred forms" of fear that were so rampant then. In the Big Book Bill W. spoke of the indescribable feeling of being rescued from a sinking ship. All we have to do is think back to the final episode of our active addiction to be filled with gratitude for our Higher Power and the gift of freedom. We smile, too, when we recall the pink cloud and those days when it seemed as though our troubles were over for good. Recovery was going to be a simple thing.

Our smile may take on a little twist, though, when we recall the time we fell off the cloud and discovered that our recovery had just begun. What followed was nothing less than the journey into the Steps—the inventory ordeal of the Fourth Step, the release of the Fifth, and the satisfaction of carrying the message. The giddy high of the pink cloud was gradually replaced by a more lasting, grounded sense of serenity and well-being as we found ourselves settling in for the long haul, one day at a time.

APPROACHING THE CROSSROADS

But what happens if we have been working the Steps diligently, going to meetings regularly, and using our sponsors, yet find that nothing positive has taken the place of the crash? We are abstinent, but recovery feels more like the absence of pain than the addition of joy. Or perhaps we find that somehow we have gradually lost touch with whatever serenity we had gained, only to find it has been replaced with a gnawing sense of restlessness and dis-ease.

Fortunately, there are many tried and true strategies for working with these scenarios. It can be as simple as going back to the basics, re-reading the texts, taking a deeper look at the first three Steps, or adding a meeting or two weekly. Sometimes seekers follow the advice given in the Big Book and find a church that feels right. Or we seek out a therapist who can support us on our Twelve Step journey. Returning to treatment, or going for the first time, is often a viable option.

Entering therapy can be a major turning point, especially if the focus is on what has come to be called family-of-origin work. This can open the door on our adult-child patterns, our codependence, our childhood abuse, and all those dysfunctional family issues that we discover underlie our addictions. Just making these new discoveries can be a real boost to our practice. We find ourselves on the trail of our addictions, tracing abuses all the way back to birth. And often we discover that this is enough. We are rewarded with the sense of well-being and serenity we have been looking for, and begin to get a glimpse of what it means to be happy, joyous, and free.

But sometimes things do not turn out according to this happy script. After all the therapy, after examining every nuance of our relationships with our mother and father over and over again, we still feel that sense of dis-ease. After uncovering perhaps four or five more addictions, somehow that joy of openness and surrender remains elusive, just out of reach. We find we are like the little Dutch boy who had to put his finger in the hole in the dike to keep it from breaking. The only difference is that we have all our fingers and toes in holes, desperately holding back the tide of addictions, while more and more holes appear.

At this point, many seekers grasp at attractive-sounding methods that promise just the sort of relief they are hoping to find. And for a while they seduce themselves into feeling they have at last left their dilemma far behind. But all too soon, these seekers, if they are fortunate, discover that they have "bought into" some brand of "pop" psychology or psuedospiritual trip which, in the end, leaves them even more disillusioned and confused. The less fortunate ones may not find their way back.

As we look back at the evolution of our recovery, there are usually a few high-water marks, which signal quantum leaps in our progress. This crisis we are discussing is one of our biggest. It is monumental because, in a very real sense, the entire thrust of our future practice hangs in the balance. Some of the roads we can take might even lead us out of the program altogether.

This can be a desperate time. We have been so diligent and thorough, and yet things still don't get better. A persistent inner voice tells us that we must be doing it wrong. Or worse, the old shaming judge within announces that there must be something inherently wrong with us. Perhaps we are not surrendering properly. Maybe we think we need to add another meeting—except we have already done this, and there is no more time in the day anyway. Or we check our insurance to see if we used up our mental health coverage the last time we went to treatment.

Whatever our minds tell us, our feelings are loud and clear. Along with the unsettling confusion, many of us report a sense of disillusionment. Those bright hopes and seemingly rock-solid convictions we had during the early days may be shaken. If we are inclined toward depression, then the depression may be all the worse. If our usual orientation to life is more on the aggressive side, then we may respond to the confusion with anger.

QUESTIONS

But through this painful time, our sense of low self-esteem is magnified. We see people smiling in meetings. We are sure that we are supposed to be experiencing the Promises by now. Why is it not happening for us? Instead of enjoying that wonderful sense of connection with the fellowship, we feel only more isolated. Once again, the specter of failure haunts us.

Then comes the fear. Here is how many report it: if we are beginning to arrive at the dreaded conclusion that we are unable to work our program correctly, then the possibility of relapse becomes very real. Obviously, this can be terrifying. But we can also begin to have doubts about the program itself. Maybe it really *is* limited. If it is, where do we go from here? It feels as though the one thing that has provided the only security we have ever known is about to abandon us. Once again the unknown threatens. Has this all been for nothing?

As we find ourselves at this dark crossroads, we begin to ask the final question, Is this all there is? It really seems to sum up the crisis. If we are coming to believe that the answer to this question is yes, then we are faced with some painful choices.

First of all, we could settle for less. We could somehow accept what we feel are the limitations of the program, put a ceiling on our expectations, and resolve to be abstinent, if not exactly happy, joyous, and free. Second, we could leave the program and find some other path that we feel might provide the answers we are looking for. How many times have we heard people say, "The Steps weren't enough, so I moved on"? Third—and we hope few would ever consider this an option—we might return to our familiar hell and try to ride the beast just one more time.

THE UNANSWERED CRY FOR HELP

The crisis is often made worse by the confusing messages we receive from our peers in the program, and even from our sponsors. Have you ever been in the middle of some very real pain, over which you had been working the Steps repeatedly, and then someone you trusted told you, "Just turn it over"? Have you ever wondered just what "turn it over" means? And have you ever tried to do it?

Thankfully, turning it over *does* work sometimes. We get the intuition that the problem has been removed by our Higher Power through our surrender. I believe, however, that we can truly turn something over, or let it go, only if we have really faced it first, embraced it, and accepted it in all its nature. There seems to be a natural order to the letting-go process. We cannot let go of something we have not truly held. If we think we can just turn it over before we come to know its nature, we are putting the cart before the horse.

Unfortunately, this sort of practice happens all too often around meeting tables. When many of us approach our sponsors or other confidants, we are told that our restlessness is the thing to be turned over. But what if the exact opposite should happen? What if, instead of surrendering *up* the dis-ease, we need to surrender *to* it? What if the dis-ease is a signal that something much deeper is trying to show itself? And what if, instead of letting it go, we need to welcome it until it reveals to us what its purpose is? If we try to let go of the disease, we are essentially repressing or avoiding the one thing we may really need to address.

Still, we usually try to turn it over. Somehow we know that surrender is a grace, but we figure there must be something we can do to help the Higher Power out a little bit. But in the end, when everything we have tried fails, we seem to arrive at the logical and inescapable conclusion that it is we ourselves who are failures.

Feeling more and more desperate, we study the words of the Big Book thumpers. We are told to "keep it simple," slow down, or that we are trying too hard. Or perhaps we are dismissed with the catch-all "dry drunk" diagnosis. Of course, frequently they are right. We remember all those times we went back to the basics, and it worked. This is not a session of program or sponsor bashing. We are absolutely convinced that our lives have been saved by the program. Many seekers may never go through any of these experiences. If this is the case, then they will continue working the program in the manner that feels right to them, and none of this need have any meaning for them. But even if there is only one person who can identify with what we have been describing, that one should be heard and given validation too.

So we listen with open minds to our friends and sponsors to be sure that what they have told us might not be valid. They have been right before. But this time, everything feels different. There is a terrible battleground inside us as we struggle to reconcile the tried and true teachings which have brought us this far with the calling of a new deep urge that feels authentic and somehow mightily important.

But perhaps the most subversive pitfall of the crossroads crisis is that we are unable to grasp that we truly *are* at a crossroads, that we actually *do* have a viable alternative to our present state. So far, hopelessness pervades all the choices we have considered. Whichever way we turn, we can see no light down the long roads. We are blocked by our fears, our confusions, and, yes, even sometimes by our own support system, which is just unable to validate us in taking what may seem to be a radical step.

This, then, is what we mean when we speak of being at the crossroads. In one sense, it is completely unknown territory. Yet in another, something about it feels totally familiar. If we think back, were we not at a crossroads when we came to our first meeting or walked into treatment that first day? Our life was on the line then, although we may not have known it. We could have chosen other paths—even insanity or death. But at that crossroads, through the mystery of grace, we chose to live instead.

And what about all those choices we have made since those first few shaky hours? Again and again, our Higher Power brings us to other crossroads. Each time we reenact the drama of the crisis and somehow make a choice for freedom, for life. Each decision is accompanied by struggle—by doubt, confusion, and fear. Each requires us to trust ourselves to the Power that has brought us this far. In a sense, each crossroads is a battleground, where we war with our moment-to-moment decision to hold on or to let go.

The hard fact is that we will be required by our own willingness to face many important crossroads, not just when we come into the program, but throughout the evolution of our practice as well. And the episode characterized by the question, Is this all there is? turns out to be one of the most important we will ever encounter.

WE ARE NOT ALONE

Sometimes we recovering people exhibit a peculiar sense of isolationism, or class consciousness. We speak of "earth people," as though we ourselves are not from earth; or else, if we are, we are somehow special. Of course, addiction does separate us from the rest of humanity in some very important ways. But more than separating us, it actually connects us to a wonderful group within the human family that has been a vital part of world culture throughout history. This group is the fellowship of persons who have chosen, for whatever reason, to pursue some form of spiritual practice.

They have existed in every culture, every walk of life, in every time and place. We know some of them by their significant contributions. But the vast majority of them are just like us—quietly going about their days, attempting to base their lives on spiritual principles, using the practices that have emerged for them uniquely and individually and that fit their cultures and times. The languages are frequently different. The steps of each practice may seem worlds apart. But the principles of each system, if we were to take a look at them, are remarkably similar. And one of the common denominators among them all is the crisis at the crossroads.

If only we could understand that this place which we believe is uniquely our own is known to many on this and every path toward wholeness! In the literature of the world's cultures, stories and myths abound of how heroes and heroines have faced this very same challenge. In one metaphor, it is called "the dark night of the soul." In many cultures, this crisis is an expected cycle in the coming of age of its members. Each society has developed rituals and practices to aid seekers on their journeys toward wholeness, just as we use the Twelve Steps.

But what does this have to do with our own dilemma, right here in the 1990s? How can knowing this make our crossroads decision any easier? First, and probably most important, it means we are not alone. We can begin to see ourselves as part of humanity in a way we had not thought of before. Our sense of belonging can extend beyond the fellowship of recovering addicts to include people from all over the world, from many different times.

This expanded connectedness can add a heroic quality to our journey. If we can examine how others have succeeded in passing through this crisis, we just may find that our Steps are not that much different from their paths. Discovering that other practices are similar to our own does not threaten the value of what we have been given. Instead, it validates our search. It can deepen our understanding, opening doorways onto new insights, which then enrich the practice of the Twelve Steps in our lives.

THERE IS MORE

All of a sudden, a new way may reveal itself at the crossroads. Instead of only confusion and darkness, which is all we have seen so far, we may find that there is a light down one of these paths after all. What seemed like desolation, losing contact with our Higher Power, might miraculously be transformed into that Power's blessing, bestowed on us in a way we could not have dreamed of before. We may just begin to believe that we have been unerringly guided to the crossroads. And now that we have arrived, we will definitely not be deserted.

Ultimately, we might be able to envision the possibility of a new answer emerging to the question, Is this all there is? And that answer will be no. There is more—a whole lot more. The best news is that this whole lot more is all within the Steps. But to understand how this is so might require us to change, at a significant level, just how we understand the Steps and recovery itself. *We will not have to abandon the method that brought us here.* We just may begin to see the Steps open up, and the Broad Highway stretch before us—the path we have always been on, and the one we will take again at the crossroads and beyond.

But for those of us who are at the crossroads now, maybe this message of hope sounds a little like fantasy. Perhaps it seems too frightening to take another new step down this mystery road without first being given some realistic encouragement, as well as some practical guidelines, on how we should actually go about making the journey. This is exactly what the next few chapters will do. After that, we can begin to make this exciting new Twelve Step practice a reality.

CHAPTER TWO

Good News—Doing It Right

One must be restless for God.

—Ramakrishna

The process of enlightenment is usually slow. But, in the end, our seeking always brings a finding.

—Bill W.

Recovering persons are well acquainted with paradox: surrendering to win, giving it away to keep it. So it might come as no surprise that the impasse we have just described in chapter 1 has another side as well. For those who have reported that sense of dis-ease, that feeling of stuckness, and who are asking the question, Is this all there is? there is good news.

Having uncomfortable feelings has meant for many of us that we were doing something wrong. Perhaps we thought we needed to work the Steps harder. Maybe we felt we were not surrendering properly or turning it over enough. It probably has never dawned on us that this feeling of dis-ease might actually be a positive signal coming to us from our Higher Power. The message could very well be that we are on the right track as the direct result of working our program really well. What a switch this is from our old idea that if we feel bad, we must be doing something wrong. It certainly is a piece of good news to know that uncomfortable feelings could mean that we are actually doing it right.

This old idea can be pretty difficult to let go of absolutely. How can having uncomfortable feelings be a sign that our program is working? Do you remember Father Martin's "chalk talk" on the Twelve Steps? When Father Martin discussed the Seventh Step, "Humbly asked Him to remove our shortcomings," he wanted to explain just how the Higher Power might actually remove our defects. He talked about asking our Higher Power for patience. In a humorous way, he demonstrated how most of us think that our Higher Power will just miraculously make us patient.

In fact, what really happens is that our Higher Power brings us experiences that show us how *impatient* we are so we can face this emotion. Therefore, when we are experiencing a greater degree of impatience than usual, it is a sign that we are actually working more effectively with the problem.

Either we are aware of the patterns of our character defects or we are unconscious of their existence. Part of the recovery process is that our character defects emerge into our awareness. When they come up for us, we say that they are on the way out. If they remain unconscious or somehow locked in place deep within us, we cannot work with them. Therefore, if the pattern has emerged, even though we may be feeling uncomfortable emotions, the defect is in the process of being removed.

In a similar way, our worst time in our active addiction, or hitting bottom, can also be seen as the closest to healing we can get before we take the First Step. In one sense, it is the "sickest" we have ever been. That is why treatment professionals try to increase the pain in order for their clients to take the First Step. Yet it gives us our best chance at recovery. The darkest hour is just before the dawn.

Taking our recovery seriously, we have been working the Steps, maintaining abstinence, and facing our underlying problems stemming from experiences that go all the way back to our earliest days—our biographical issues. If we still experience the sense of what one spiritual teacher has called "celestial nostalgia," it means that we are actually deep in the process of recovery, not avoiding it. It means our Higher Power has brought us uncomfortable states of being in direct response to our willingness to surrender to that Power and to the process of recovery itself.

This attitude can completely transform the way we think of

Twelve Step practice. We come to realize that the sense of disease is not something to be turned over or let go of, but somehow surrendered to and embraced, even in its uncomfortableness. "Pain is the touchstone of spiritual progress," we are told in the Twelve and Twelve.* Let us touch it, then, and see it for what it really is—the way-show-er, the catalyst, perhaps even a gift.

We are not discounting our feelings here. Pain hurts. We are not suggesting that we suppress or deny the intensity of our emotions. Many of us have become disillusioned with approaches that give us platitudes about how we do not have to hurt. Ultimately, that type of self-help adds up to avoidance of legitimate struggle. But *seeing pain in this new light gives it meaning.* It provides a context for it. It is the difference between pointless struggle and meaningful struggle.

Birth is the best example. It is one of the most painful experiences some women ever have; we even call it "labor." Yet, many women say that no experience could be more fulfilling. This type of suffering signals the emergence of something wonderful. In recovery, our struggles can mean this too. In a sense, we too are being born anew into a new self, a new way of being.

Truly understanding pain as a sign of doing it right is not something that will happen overnight. It takes quite awhile to change the lifelong habit of always thinking we are doing it wrong, or worse, of *being* wrong. But if we can begin to practice this new idea and add it to our worldview, we can gradually let go of the old one. What a relief to discover that we are working our program really well!

THE "X-FACTOR"—THE HIGHER POWER IN RECOVERY

Do you remember the research that came out a few years ago on the physical cause of alcoholism? It seems that scientists had isolated some fascinating physical evidence—endorphins, chromosomes, and biochemicals. But there was a missing piece in the equation, something they were unable to measure. They called it the "X-factor." If you think about it, this is a pretty humorous

---

*Twelve Steps and Twelve Traditions (New York: A.A. World Services, Inc., 1981).

admission—that there is something about addiction they just plain don't know but are acting as if they do anyway.

For us in recovery, there is an ever-present X-factor in our lives as well. This X-factor is the Higher Power. We learn a few things about our Higher Power by experiencing the results of working the Steps in our lives. In fact, we may go so far as to say that our entire recovery is based on developing and improving our relationship with this Power.

Yet since the 1930s, when the founding members of AA began to talk about a Higher Power, that Power has remained a mystery. We experience that it can remove obsession and compulsion. We also experience that this Power works through the Steps to gradually remove our character defects, allowing us to have healthy relationships with family and friends.

But what else might this Power do? What are its limits? Does it even have any? What does it mean to "let go absolutely" or, as it also says in the Big Book, "abandon ourselves"? When Bill W. spoke of being "rocketed into the fourth dimension," was he just being poetic, or was he really onto something—perhaps talking about a real place in our consciousness that we all have access to?

We have seen ourselves change emotionally and psychologically. But are we ever supposed to say "enough"? Do we say, "I've let go absolutely, as much as I'm going to. I have to hold on to *something*"?

I was one of those on a pink cloud early in my Twelve Step practice. I remember spreading my arms wide to the Higher Power and professing total willingness and absolute surrender. Then, when my Steps got me down to business, that undying commitment to willingness turned into "Never mind; I take it back," or "Let's think about this a little bit." I had no idea while riding the cloud what real in-depth exploration would look like.

Could it be that our Higher Power, through the Steps, has brought us to a far boundary of our program—almost to this jumping-off place—all because we have made the decision, deeper than we realize, to turn our lives over?

In ancient Greece and Egypt and other places, there were spiritual societies called "mystery schools." In a mystery school, members of the society practiced the outer, more easily grasped teachings until they were ready for the hidden, deeper side of the discipline. Old writings speak of such times of readiness as being "at the door of the temple," "entering the holy of holies," or "the secret rites." Could it be that the Twelve Step program is like these ancient mystery schools and that many of us are preparing to step into the next, deeper level?

From the experience of those who have gone through this stage seems to be emerging a truth that can be worded like this: *The natural and inevitable result of using the Higher Power in our lives through daily application of the Steps is that we will enter an uncharted and heretofore unknown part of ourselves, which we can only call "spiritual."* We will move through the door of the temple.

AT THE DOOR

Realizing we are at the door can be frightening. For one thing, as we mentioned earlier, we just do not know of any language that accurately describes what spirituality is. We all know something about religion, but that type of language does not come close to describing what is happening. Feeling this unrest, and coming to believe that a Higher Power might be taking us over the edge, we worry that we may relapse or perhaps even go crazy. We know from our experiences in active addiction how to get "out there," or actually go over the edge. We may even remember glimpses of something that felt spiritual while we were in our mood-altered states. But clean and sober now, we have often put a wall between us and anything that has to do with changing consciousness.

There is often little support for being at this crossroads. We are told to "keep it simple" or "turn it over." These time-honored sayings on the walls of meeting halls are always important, but they sometimes can be used as an avoidance, or even a crutch. For example, I remember when restlessness began to be an everyday thing for me. I was told to turn it over. The message I was getting was that if I were working my program right, I would not be feeling restless. So I used my will to push away the restlessness. Yet it still persisted. For me, this meant one of two things: either I was a failure at surrender, or my Higher Power was bringing me the restlessness as a catalyst to encourage me to improve my conscious contact. I found out that I was not supposed to let go of it, but embrace it, look at it, and learn from it what message it was trying to give me.

Sometimes we fall into the trap of feeling extra guilt and shame. Many of us have done good psychological work by dealing with codependence and family-of-origin issues and going to therapy. We have been like bloodhounds on the trail of our addictions, sniffing them out one by one. Yet there always seems to be one more just around the next bend. The unrest stays. Where do we go when we have searched every nook and cranny of our childhood time and time again and still long for something else?

Let us look at the crisis in light of this new way of thinking. The best possible result of turning our lives over to the Higher Power is that we will literally have to let go of our old ideas—not just some of them, but all of them. We are finding that our program means business—that surrender is deeper than we have ever dreamed, and that there just may be a few more First Steps we have to take. What's more, we are discovering that resisting the lead of our Higher Power might be the very cause of our unrest to begin with. Carl Jung has said that addiction is a "thirst for wholeness." If that is the case, then no wonder we continue to crave something more. Perhaps there are expanding horizons of wholeness that we have yet to discover.

Though this may seem like a frightening and sometimes lonely time, there is more good news. Many others have reached the same place in their recovery. And there is plenty of help for those who choose to undertake what Joseph Campbell has called "the Hero's Journey." Many books and methods are available to provide language for spirituality. Many support groups exist that can guide us as well. Bill W. spoke of the "treasure trove" of aids available to us and invited us to seek them out. Remember, we have the founding members' blessing in our search. The blessing is in the Big Book and the Twelve and Twelve. We are advised to avail ourselves of medicine, religion, and psychiatry.

And don't forget the most important encouragement of all—the Eleventh Step. We are told to seek to improve conscious contact with our Higher Power, using prayer and meditation. This is our invitation, directly from the Steps, to use whatever methods we can to fulfill the intention of the Step. It is our own open-door policy. We have carte blanche to explore spirituality.

Many people have said, "The Steps aren't big enough. I need something more." I believe this is a limited perspective. There is a larger interpretation than this. The lovely thing is that our search, which at first glimpse seems outside the program and the Steps, is actually an integral part of them. Since the Steps say to do what we must to improve conscious contact, using any other discipline actually just enriches the Steps.

I also believe it is a misunderstanding to say that the Steps and the Big Book *are* enough. That's true in a way, but if you take the book and the Steps literally, they tell us to go elsewhere. They actually sanction our entire search, no matter where it takes us. In fact, rigidly confining our search to what is between the covers of the text is like deliberately turning our backs on the gift that is offered. We speak frequently about addictive denial. But is it possible that we could be in denial of our spiritual potential as well?

In the literature of the East, there are many works that describe something called the Tao. Although the Tao defies definition in any language, it is sometimes described as "the Way." The Way is the universal practice of moving toward wholeness, or living life spiritually. It is more than just a religion, more, even, than a spiritual practice. The Tao is said to be so all-encompassing that all our lives and seeking are part of it. We are coming to believe that the Steps are like this Tao—are part of the Tao. We will cover in detail in later chapters how this might be so.

But for now, we can say that the Steps are infinitely vast and give us unending leeway to pursue our practice of them. If we can have faith in our Higher Power, if we continually make the decision to trust and to turn our lives over, then we can rest assured that we will be guided to follow the path of the Steps deeper than we ever have before.

So instead of despairing that we have reached the limit of the Steps, we can now celebrate that they are revealing a greater depth of themselves. We are also excited that beyond the Twelve Step movement, there is an extended fellowship of support from psychology, philosophy, and even science to help make the journey more fulfilling.

The pioneers said, "We realize we know only a little. God will constantly disclose more to you and to us." I believe this is happening now. We would be denying our chance to grow in our recovery if we turned our backs on what our Higher Power might be revealing to us.

In the next chapter we will begin to take a look at what happens when the radical rearrangement that Carl Jung said was required for recovery happens again. Just how old are old ideas, and how do individuals, as well as societies, deal with the profound shifts in thinking that seem to turn everything upside down? Then, in later chapters, we can discuss in more detail this mysterious thing called spirituality. We may even demystify the language somewhat by showing how various disciplines describe these types of experiences.

CHAPTER THREE

New Ideas—Living in a Different World

. . . deep down in every man, woman, and child is the fundamental idea of God.

—Bill W.

It is an almost ridiculous prejudice to assume that existence can only be physical.

—Carl Jung

The farther limits of our being plunge, it seems to me, into an altogether other dimension of existence from the sensible and merely "understandable" world. Name it the mystical region, or the supernatural region, whichever you choose.

—William James

I was in another world, a new world of consciousness.

—Bill W.

THE NATURE OF PARADIGMS

When we think of growing in recovery, most often we think of the way we feel—how some painful emotions have been transformed into their more constructive counterparts—fear into courage, shame into self-love. Or we point to the way we have developed a growing acceptance of the universality of these painful feelings and have learned how to be with them in more creative ways.

We also speak of changing old habits—ways of doing things, the words we say—and developing new responses to replace the dysfunctional ones. And of course there are the words from the Big Book read thousands of times a day in meetings throughout the world: "Some of us have tried to hold on to our old ideas and the result was nil until we let go absolutely." So it becomes extremely important for us to include this letting go of old ideas and then somehow to allow our Higher Power, working through the Steps, to replace them with new ones.

It is painful when we are the collision point between old ideas dying and new ones being born. But we might gain some perspective on this pain when we learn that this battleground of old and new ideas is a major theme occupying science and many other disciplines, including psychology, today. Understanding how these crises work at the collective level of humanity can prove to be extremely enlightening as we prepare to take our individual journey deeper into the Steps. Whereas we in recovery talk about letting go of old ideas and the struggle this causes, philosophy now speaks of changing a *group* of ideas, called a *paradigm*, and of the collision that happens when two paradigms overlap.

A common recovery issue illustrates what a paradigm is and how it can affect our lives. When I began to do my family-of-origin, codependence, and adult-child work, I realized how I felt responsible for just about everything that went on around me, especially things that happened in my family of origin. Naturally, I felt shame, guilt, and low self-esteem as the result of carrying this weight. I will never forget my reaction the first time my therapist told me I was not responsible for my family. She told me I did not have to take care of them and that I did not cause them to be unhappy.

I was in shock. I literally could not accept this. Feeling responsible was such an ingrained part of me, so basic, so inherent, that she might as well have told me that all this time I had been living on Mars instead of Earth. It was that alien to me. I could not imagine a life where I did not feel responsible. It was as real to me as breath. Yet over the years, I am gradually coming to see that feeling responsible is not a condition of reality per se, but an idea or concept *about* reality that I somehow took on for myself. It is just that it was so close to me, so ingrained and such a part of my core, that I thought that it *was* reality.

I now realize that my entire worldview was shaped by and bound to this idea that I held deep within my consciousness. This idea about reality had great power because it totally shaped, and helped to create, the rest of my years—how I related to people, how I acted and felt, and how I responded to life's problems.

This, then, is a paradigm. A paradigm is a worldview—a way of acting, thinking, and feeling in the world—based on an idea, or a group of ideas, about the world. However, a paradigm is *not* the world. But it can be so pervasive that it is almost impossible to realize that it is *not* reality or the truth, but only one way of *looking at* reality. A paradigm also has great power to sustain itself, because there seems to be some sort of built-in mechanism that limits thinking or exploration outside itself.

Let's use another example to illustrate how paradigms operate in a more global way to affect the lives of millions of people. This next one not only shows how a paradigm or worldview orders the subsequent flow of events, but also reveals a more subversive dynamic. There is a strong investment in a paradigm to remain unchanged, as well as a tendency for the followers of a paradigm to feel threatened by new ideas that challenge the prevailing view.

The history of the automobile industry provides a case in point. Since Henry Ford built the first car, there have been amazing advances in automobile design and engine performance. Just take a look at a picture of a Model T alongside the new Jaguar. But no matter how fast or sleek the automobile has become—even though there is an almost jet-like sophistication to the dashboard—plush leather, gold plate, real wood styling—even with all these advances, incredible as it may seem, an automobile still has the basic engine design that was invented ninety years ago. Cars are still piston-driven, internal combustion machines and, most profoundly, they still run on fossil fuel. Whether your car cost $495 off a junk pile or $97,000 from Italy, you still have to pump gas. Gasoline is a core-ordering principle of the automobile paradigm. This fundamental concept controls the thought of the most sophisticated engineers, the flow of billions of dollars, and, indeed, the entire world economy.

We all know of alternative ways to run cars—with electricity, methane, and the like. We dare not speculate as to why we are not developing these technologies. But one thing seems fairly obvious. There is an enormous investment by some of the world's most powerful industries, as well as the insatiable thirst for oil of the world's economies, to effectively straitjacket any concerted attempt to provide viable alternatives. You get the picture? Perhaps now it is easier to see how the power of a paradigm inhibits thought outside itself, as well as sustains itself against any changes that threaten its existence. It is hard to imagine what planet Earth would be like without gasoline-powered automobiles.

THE PARADOX

When we speak of letting go of our old ideas, most of us think of letting go of thoughts or concepts. Even if they are extremely deep—even unconscious, like my old responsibility paradigm—we can conceive of the possibility of changing them. We imagine ourselves as individual thinkers, or units of awareness or consciousness. Although our thoughts change, we as thinkers seem to remain the same.

But here is where it gets fascinating. What happens when the *thinker* changes? Read these words of Bill W. as he describes his spiritual experience:

> *The light, the ecstasy—I was conscious of nothing else for a time period. . . . I stood upon a summit where a great wind blew. A wind, not of air, but of spirit . . . I seemed to be possessed by the absolute.*

What do we make of it? Is it a hallucination or a vision? This certainly does not sound like ordinary consciousness. He speaks of the wind of spirit blowing—of being on a mountain. Well, where is he? Is the real Bill W. in the hospital room or on the mountain? What's going on here? We get the notion that this must be the thing that Carl Jung was talking about in the Big Book. Jung said that no psychology could heal an alcoholic. The only thing that might work was what he called a radical "rearrangement" of consciousness. This is the conversion experience. At other times, it is called a spiritual awakening or spiritual experience. Something more than just thoughts are changed. Our entire way of operating as a human being—our whole identity—shifts. And in general, there are no adequate words to describe such a shift. The Big Book says it can be gradual or sudden. Most people resort to symbols or metaphors when they try to explain it. They say, "It was like a . . ." or "I felt as though . . ." or something like this.

Later we will go into more detail about spiritual awakenings and spiritual experiences. We will explore the many ways people today and for all time have had such experiences, and how amazingly prevalent they are. This can help us define spirituality for ourselves in a way that makes sense.

As with Bill W., what many of us are experiencing is validated by some of the most sophisticated and advanced contemporary thinkers. They have already begun to find a language for spirituality, as well as a practical basis for the radical rearrangement. Just how can Bill W. exist as a "skin-encapsulated ego," as Alan Watts said, and at the same time be part of "the wind of spirit" on the mountaintop or "possessed by the absolute"? It does not seem possible that these two things can exist at the same time. But, surprisingly enough, psychologists, philosophers, and scientists say that such a paradox is plausible.

AT THE CROSSROADS—PSYCHOLOGY AND SPIRITUALITY

In addition to being spiritual, the Twelve Steps are certainly a psychological system. Ask anybody who has done a Fourth or Fifth Step. We usually feel pretty good about using some sort of psychology if we feel it might support our practice of the Steps. But for us in recovery, traditional psychology, as it has unfolded since Freud's time, poses one unavoidable dilemma. Basically, most current psychological theory states that a spiritual experience is a sign of pathology. Spiritual experiences are seen as the repression or avoidance of early childhood trauma. It goes without saying, then, that there has been little language in psychology to describe spirituality in anything but negative terms.

One quickly sees how this sort of thinking straitjackets practitioners of the Twelve Steps. We are basing our lives on spirituality. Yet we also feel it is important, as the Big Book points out, to do some supportive psychological work. This has been a distressingly prevalent problem in treatment centers, which seem to have a lot of psychological expertise, but in general much less ability to adequately support recovering persons on the spiritual journey—other than to talk about how we need to "have spirituality." To say that spirituality is required for recovery but that spirituality is a sickness is a catch-22.

Fortunately, this is not the only perspective in psychology. The founder of the humanistic psychology movement, Abraham Maslow, offered another approach when he presented his research on "peak experiences." He was among the first in modern psychology to advocate that the spiritual experience was a sign of *health*, not pathology. Finally, there was actual psychological validation and support for spirituality.

Later, Maslow was among those who took the frontiers of psychology even further. Along with Anthony Sutich, Stanislav Grof, and others, he was a founder of transpersonal psychology, the field's latest force. For us in the West, who have grown up in the Freudian psychological tradition yet who are feeling this thing that Carl Jung called the "thirst for wholeness," transpersonal psychology has proven to be a valuable support and resource. For the first time we have available to us a discipline that bridges the traditional understanding of Freud and his successors with the spiritual philosophies and religions of the world—what Aldous Huxley has called the "perennial philosophy." Because transpersonal psychology includes spirituality, it has obvious value for Twelve Step practitioners. It is also providing fascinating maps of what this fourth dimension we got "rocketed" into might look like.

Transpersonal psychology is valuable not just because it has developed a theoretical framework, but also because it provides methods that can help seekers *experience* spirituality. Hence, these have been called "experiential" modalities. Many of us say that these modalities are Eleventh Step methods—ways we can improve our conscious contact. In a later chapter, we will lay out this banquet table of techniques—some brand-new and others time-honored. We will also explore the influence of William James and Carl Jung on the Twelve Steps and how the Twelve Steps have always had deep spiritual and transpersonal roots.

Again, many on the brink of despair can feel excitement and hope. It feels like a spiritual experience itself to realize that we are not crazy but rather are in the company of some of the greatest psychologists the world has yet produced.

THE PARTICLE AND THE WAVE— SCIENCE AND SPIRITUALITY

Even though new insights in psychology help make spirituality more understandable to seekers, it is the science of the twentieth century that may give it the most credibility. If anything has represented the no-nonsense, practical, and logical side of our culture, it is science, with its brainchild, technology, and its grandparent, the entire Western rational way of thinking. So when scientists themselves begin to tread the realm of spirituality, people pay attention.

Fritjof Capra is a contemporary scientist who has popularly conceptualized the way modern physics resembles ancient spiritual systems. In his book *The Tao of Physics*, Capra uses the term *Newtonian-Cartesian paradigm*. This term characterizes the worldview that has dominated science and, subsequently, all Western disciplines, including psychology, for the last three hundred years. He explores the paradigm collision that is now occurring and some of the latest principles of physics and other sciences. These clashes are signaling that even within the rigorous disciplines of hard science, nothing is absolute anymore.

Let's take a look at this traditional Western worldview and then explore two revolutionary physics principles that represent the new scientific paradigm currently emerging. With these as a backdrop, we can then show how this paradigm collision mirrors the very same dilemma we are now facing in our recovery.

Capra used the scientist Isaac Newton and the philosopher Rene Descartes to name the Western worldview, although he might just as well have used many other figures. Basically, Western science adopted Newton's belief that the universe was a very complex machine composed of miniature physical objects, or atoms. All understanding of this universe as a mechanism could be determined from studying the relationship between these particles.

To this mechanistic understanding Descartes added the principle that there is a fundamental separation between mind and matter. This has come to be called the philosophy of dualism. Basically, Descartes said that the individual self, the "I," was the only reality of which humans could be certain. And the faculty which guaranteed this sense of reality was human reason. This dualism can also be seen as the separation between subject and object, humanity and nature, and matter and spirit.

Before this time, many cultures throughout history believed that God, or the Divine, existed in humanity, in nature, and in every part of the universe. It was generally maintained that there was a higher office of truth than just the human intellect. Moreover, the whole universe was somehow "alive," or endowed with divine power. But Descartes said that though God created the universe, He existed outside of it. The universe itself was a lifeless machine governed by a few laws that could be understood and manipulated by the power of human reason. This basic idea became the fundamental tenet of Western science.

Descartes actually concretized what Aristotle and some other Greek philosophers had already formulated. Indeed, some modern philosophers have traced dualism to the Old Testament, where there is a strong emphasis on duality—heaven and earth, man and nature, God-good and devil-evil, and matter and spirit.

The mechanistic-dualistic worldview, or the belief that the universe is a machine and that there is an unbridgeable separation between matter and spirit, contradicts virtually all other world philosophies since the beginning of history. Almost every culture before this time has viewed reality in terms of wholeness, albeit in extremely diverse metaphors. Most proposed an underlying unity in creation. All parts of the whole were seen as being interrelated or connected with each other, and a function of the whole—indeed the whole itself. Even though on one level matter and spirit are apparently different, on another level matter is actually infused with spirit or is just another form that the original spirit can take.

One way to demonstrate the difference between the Newtonian-Cartesian worldview and the holistic paradigm of other world societies is to take a look at an often-used metaphor. A common theme that describes the relationship between mind and matter, subject and object, or the individual and the universe is that of the wave and the ocean. The wave is seen as the part, which is somehow individual, yet at the same time identical to, and none other than, the ocean. The ocean is seen as the whole, or the All. Also, the wave can be viewed as matter and the ocean as spirit. Today we in the West often speak of this philosophy as an Eastern worldview. But in fact, native cultures and preindustrial civilizations in all hemispheres have also used this perspective.

Thinkers from the holistic tradition would argue that even though the wave and the ocean are different *in form*, they are the same *in substance*. Both the wave and the ocean are composed of water, or H_2O. If we were to examine under a microscope a drop of water from a wave or a drop from the ocean itself, the composition of the two drops would be identical. Yet, *at the same time*, a wave and the ocean have different characteristics that give each its individuality. In this way, the simultaneous oneness of and difference between the wave and the ocean demonstrate a paradox that seems to contradict the very basis of rational thought. Difference and identity can coexist in one philosophy. Matter and spirit, subject and object, and God and the universe are not forever separate parts but have a component of oneness.

From the Newtonian-Cartesian point of view, this type of holistic thinking is false. Western scientific observers would argue that according to *reason*, this philosophy contradicts itself and proposes an inherently irreconcilable paradox. How can the part and the whole be identical and different at the same time? Something is either one thing or it is another. It cannot be two contradictory things at once. It either *is* or it *is not*. Because the holistic worldview seems so illogical and irrational, it is therefore rejected out of hand as being primitive and unscientific.

Another way to explain the difference between these two types of thinking is to say that one is linear and the other nonlinear. "Linear" implies that there is a logical, ordered process to reasoning and scientific inquiry. Thus Newtonian-Cartesian thinking can be called linear. "Nonlinear" suggests that things are not always that predictable and that life cannot be accurately described without making room for contradiction, or the element of mystery. *Holistic thinkers do not deny that linear thinking has its place*. In fact, many important scientific and philosophical principles are based on the rational approach. However, holistic thinkers also insist that for a more accurate picture of the nature of reality, there must also be a place for nonlinear, or holistic thinking.

Whereas there is room for both a linear and nonlinear approach in the philosophy of "holism," from the Newtonian-Cartesian point of view, there is no place for nonlinear thinking. In traditional Western science, there is only one true perspective: The individual, in an absolute sense, is separate from the rest of the world. The world is material and is made of separate objects.

This philosophy has been of immeasurable importance and accounts for most of the scientific and technological advances of the twentieth century. However, it is ultimately only *one way* to look at reality. Its basic limitation is that there is no room for any other worldview. This is what we mean when we say thinkers can be "paradigm-bound." If new information becomes available that seems to contradict the basic tenets of the paradigm, it is called unscientific. All scientific inquiry must proceed along the lines of the preordained set of assumptions.

My own belief that I was responsible for my parents was a personal worldview and a core-ordering principle of my life, *even though it was false*. In the same way, Newtonian-Cartesian thinking has acted as the shaper of all modern inquiry and action, *even though it is only one possible perspective*. It is almost as though a paradigm acts as a denial system. One cannot see outside the paradigm from within it.

A wonderful parable from an Eastern culture illustrates this point. A group of blind people were asked to describe an elephant by touching it. One person said, "An elephant is a long, very thin, rope-like creature with bushy hair at one end." A second said, "An elephant is a wide, flat, flabby thing, and not a rope at all." A third argued, "You are both wrong; an elephant is a great, solid, tree-like column." And still another said they were all crazy: "An elephant is an elegant, sweeping, bone-like creature, smooth and sharp." And the last one said, "You're all stupid. An elephant is a flexible, tapering animal that can spray water from one end and grasp peanuts."

It is obvious that they were talking about the elephant's tail, ear, leg, tusk, and trunk, respectively. They were each correct insofar as they could accurately describe their part. But they were all ignorant in that they mistook their own frames of reference as being the whole truth. Any approach that operates this blindly will miss the whole picture. The elephant is something more than just each of its parts. Reality is something more than just theories and paradigms about it. Just as in addictive denial, there is an inherent arrogance and egocentricity in paradigms that see any other worldview as wrong.

Another classic example of the clash between worldviews occurs in *Hamlet*, when Hamlet is telling his close friend, Horatio, how he has just seen his father's ghost. Horatio does not believe him and seeks to convince Hamlet that such phenomena are not real. Hamlet replies, "There are more things in heaven and earth, Horatio, than are dreamt of in your philosophy." The key here is the phrase "in your philosophy." Any philosophy goes by a set of assumptions. What the holistic paradigm is proposing is a philosophy that makes room for multiple ways of viewing reality. Only with such a broad perspective can we hope to approach anything like the true nature of the universe.

Lest we lose ourselves in scientific exploration, we can remind ourselves of why this discussion is important for us. Recovery is a radical change not just in how we behave, but also in how we think. Those of us who grew up immersed in the Western scientific way of thinking have tended to reject spirituality as unscientific and irrational. If we cannot explain it logically, or categorize it within a system of unchangeable laws, then it must not be real. This is a great stumbling block for us as we take on the spiritual practice of the Twelve Steps, which requires us to let go of old ideas.

The barrier to spirituality begins in our minds. And sometimes it feels like asking too much of ourselves to throw out science in favor of a spirituality that has no grounding within any philosophy we have ever known. What if there could be some sort of reconciliation between spirituality and science—one that would enable us to embrace spirituality while maintaining a consistent belief in at least some sound scientific principles? We want to find out if, by letting go of *some* scientific axioms, there may be another whole set that can take their place. Is it possible that these, at the same time, might more accurately reflect and support what we are discovering through our spiritual awakenings?

Amazingly, we are currently experiencing just such an expansion in scientific thinking. Twentieth-century physicists have challenged the mechanistic worldview that we are coming to see is too narrow a definition of reality. Albert Einstein's equation $E=MC^2$ demonstrated that matter was actually a form of energy. With this and other findings, scientists are beginning to tread dangerously close to principles of nondualism and spirituality as these ideas have been expressed by mystics for millennia. This is not the place to present a detailed history of the new physics. There are some good sources listed in the Bibliography that fully explore the fascinating scientific breakthroughs of this century. However, there are two concepts that effectively support and explain this revolution.

The first of these was formulated by the physicist Werner Heisenberg. As we stated, classical science was all based on the idea that the universe was a machine. This machine was a collection of objects of various size, from the enormous to the very minute, whose relationship between each other could be correctly measured. But just as Einstein demonstrated something revolutionary about matter and energy, Heisenberg also discovered something fascinating about objects, or matter itself. He found that objects do not just exist or not exist, but rather have *tendencies* or *probabilities* to exist. Along with making these observations, he also developed the "uncertainty principle."

Without getting any more scientific, we can readily see how

"unscientific" this sounds. How many times have we said, "Be logical. Either something is, or it isn't"? How often have we ourselves been rigid, somehow thinking we were being scientific? All of a sudden, here is a profound idea, actually entertained by some of the world's most brilliant minds, that includes a fundamental mystery. The uncertainty principle—what a radical idea! It sure does describe, with *certainty*, how many of us are feeling as we move deeper into the Steps.

The famous wave/particle controversy is probably most indicative of the close relationship between new science and spirituality. For years, scientists argued whether light was a particle or a wave. Some showed it to be one thing, others another, each with equal credentials and expertise. However, not until Niels Bohr's contribution was the controversy reconciled into one unified theory. Bohr formulated a principle that was totally heretical at the time. He said that light was *both* a particle *and* a wave, depending on the type of observation or how the experiment was carried out. He called this the "principle of complementarity." In other words, it was not an "either-or" situation but a "both-and." Can you grasp the mind-blowing character of this discovery? How can something be two opposite things at the same time? This is certainly not linear, not logical. Yet this type of paradox and contradiction came to be accepted in the scientific community. It is difficult to understand this kind of paradox unless you have been "rocketed into the fourth dimension."

BRINGING IT BACK HOME

How does all of this support spirituality? Basically, the admission by science of the reality of uncertainty and paradox reconciles the Western dualistic worldview and the nondualistic philosophy of the rest of the world's cultures. Instead of saying this universe is either a complex machine bound by time and space or a vast interplay of energies that make up one seamless whole, we can now say that both these realities are true.

How does this relate to the question, What is a human being? Instead of wondering whether we are an individual "I" as Descartes said, the "skin-encapsulated ego" of Alan Watts, or whether we are the Whole, the One, as the Hindus say, now we can see that *both* these positions are true. In a very complementary way, reality, the universe, and even humans have a particle nature *and* a wave nature, or a separate and a whole self. Carl Jung might say we have an individual and a collective self. Transpersonal psychologists might call it a personal and transpersonal self.

We are learning that in order to deepen our recovery, we must work with the personal self, which is what we have been doing all along anyway. But we must also realize that we have another self, the collective, our wave nature, which also enters the domain of recovery. When we begin to be conscious of our wave nature, we begin to feel the dis-ease and restlessness. The feelings are all the more acute because we have not known that this part of our nature exists. If we have begun to get hints that it does, we have not been supported in our newfound truth, or we have actually been criticized for it. As Alan Watts might say, the Newtonian-Cartesian paradigm has been a powerful taboo against knowing who you are.

Fortunately, new science, philosophy, and even psychology are saying yes to our journey. We realize that we are supported on our way. Instead of guarding the doors against our search of the world's great traditions, philosophers and even some scientists are now happily giving us the keys.

This, then, is the good news. Our dis-ease is a sign—first, that we are experiencing a paradigm collision within ourselves, and second, that we are on the right track because of this. And when, through our Higher Power, we enter the door of the temple, take the leap, or head out into the desert, we will have practical and grounded disciplines to support us. We will not be alone. There is a language for it. There is room in the program for mystery and paradox.

What we are saying is that if we use the Steps and the Higher Power diligently, our worldview will change. For a while we will live in the paradigm collision, just as the world is now involved in such a collision. We will think and feel in the way we have always thought and felt. At the same time, we will be responding to new ideas about who we are and what the universe is. Being the battleground between the old and the new causes us our pain; yet it is also a sign that we are truly answering the call of our being.

What happens if we let go absolutely? None of us knows for sure. We are uncertain. We can be sure it will feel strange and sometimes frightening. We may feel alone, unable to understand or be understood. All the ideas that we held about the Steps and about the Higher Power may change. What is required at this stage is an even greater faith. We can rely on the Third Step if we want to. We have made a decision to turn our lives over, and we must make it time and time again. Perhaps it can even become a moment-to-moment process of surrender. So if real surrender is what actually happens, why shouldn't the Higher Power be taking us on a journey into the mystery?

Fortunately for us, though, this is not a blind faith we must have, but one well-grounded in experience. It is important for us not to lose touch with the basic principles that have guided our recovery. We do not forget what active addiction is like. But probably the most important thing we can do in our recovery now is to answer this call, even if it means moving into uncharted territories. We can step a little more freely as we go forward in our search, knowing that there are many guides who have already trod what Bill W. called the Broad Highway and that just as many more walk beside us now.

CHAPTER FOUR

Back to the Source— The Power Beneath the Steps

For all the tragedy of life is caused by consciousness of self. Every pain and depression is caused by this, and anything that can take away the thought of the self helps to a certain extent to relieve man from pain; but God-consciousness gives a perfect relief.

—Hazrat Inayat Khan

To recover what is lost we must break out of the worlds of ego.

—Sri Aurobindo

Above everything, we alcoholics must be rid of this selfishness.

—Bill W.

When one of my sponsors would refer me to various Steps and program slogans, he always added an interesting twist. If we were talking about the Third Step, about making a decision to turn it over, or about surrender, he would say something like this: "You know, when a frog is sitting on a lily pad, and he makes a decision to jump, he's still sittin'. He's still gotta jump."

So far on this new adventure deeper into the Steps, we are sort of like that frog. We find ourselves at the crossroads, preparing for the journey, yet we still have not set out. We are still sitting on the lily pad. Our preparations have already revealed some important things about ourselves that should serve us well.

For one, we have found that even with all our confusion, we *are* on the right track. We have also received validation for our changing ideas about the world and reality. Why, then, do we hesitate?

Once again, I believe that our reluctance is a sign that we are working our program well. For if we are serious about recovery and if we consider it precious, then we have every right to be as convinced as possible that this new undertaking won't undermine our foundation. Perhaps we have not set out because there is one more thing we need to do.

But instead of running off on the promise of some strange-sounding philosophy, maybe it is time to take one last hard look at the foundations of the program and the Steps themselves. How does all this new information relate to our practice? Could we be changing horses in midstream? Is the journey we are about to take so radically foreign to what we hold to be inviolate that it will be almost like giving up our recovery altogether?

This is an extremely important point in this book's unfolding, as well as a momentous time on our journey. If we are considering taking the leap, we *need* to be asking questions like these. Therefore, we will look back one more time, before we head out, so that we can actually understand how the Steps and these new ideas are related.

BILL'S STORY—BETWEEN THE LINES

Going right to the source is the surest way to uncover the original meanings and intentions of the Twelve Step movement. What better place to start than with Bill W. himself? We have probably all read his story in the Big Book, and what it says is amplified significantly in his AA-authorized biography, *Pass It On*. *Pass It On* proves to be one of our most valuable resources in the search for the spiritual and psychological origins of the Twelve Steps.

In looking at Bill W.'s First Step experience, three elements are especially worth noting. First is the ongoing support he had from the medical community, especially his friend Dr. Silkworth. Nevertheless, the most revolutionary form of help came from another alcoholic, Ebby. Ebby's contact with Bill became the blueprint for Twelfth Step work.

The second pivotal element is the story of another alcoholic, Roland, who had been a patient of the psychiatrist Carl Jung. Jung made it clear to Roland that without some sort of radical rearrangement of consciousness, he could not recover. By the time Bill met him, Roland had undergone a spiritual awakening as a part of the Oxford Group, a cross-denominational Christian sect.

Another point along this same line is Bill's study of William James's *The Varieties of Religious Experience*. James is often considered the father of American psychology. Philosophy from these three sources—Carl Jung, William James, and the Oxford Group—are the primary forces beneath the Twelve Steps and the principles of Alcoholics Anonymous.

The third, and most powerful, underpinning is Wilson's own spiritual experience. His moving narrative in the Big Book is expanded with even more poetic power in *Pass It On*. I invite you to read it, if you have not already done so. If you have, then it would be refreshing to read it again. It is a classic example of mystical writing, its words describing the spiritual episode as it could be experienced by anyone in any culture, from any religion or historical period. The passage represents the most reassuring encouragement that we might hope to rely on for journeying into the deeper mysteries of spirituality. (We will go into more depth about this experience later.)

It is probably safe to say that of these pivotal influences, by far the most attention has been paid to the one that became the second part of the Twelfth Step—carrying the message. So without in any way taking away from the prominence of this dynamic, we will look more closely at some of the others. It is possible that by amplifying them, we may begin to find the answers we have been searching for.

THE OXFORD GROUP—TAKING SPIRITUALITY SERIOUSLY

There were four primary principles fostered by the Oxford Group, called the Four Absolutes: Honesty, Purity, Unselfishness, and Love. The Oxford Group was a no-nonsense fellowship that believed in the power of direct spiritual experience, as opposed to mere affiliation with a church or creed. Its aim was no less than world conversion. Members believed this goal could be accomplished by the concerted practice of prayer and meditation, by making restitution for wrongdoings, and by a zealous sharing with others on a one-to-one basis. Does this sound vaguely familiar? It is easy to see where many of the principles of the Twelve Step program originated.

Before the actual founding of AA and the writing of the Steps, Bill and the early pioneers would meet with Bill's friend Sam Shoemaker, an Oxford Group member. The newly sober alcoholics would spend a lot of time in the "upper room" on their knees, praying and meditating. There was no apology given for their unabashedly spiritual approach. They were well aware that spirituality was the key to recovery and were single-minded in their efforts to help create an atmosphere that could foster a spiritual experience.

Are you beginning to get a sense of this deep and powerful root of the program? Their one-pointedness was almost intimidating; they really meant business. Many of us can remember that when we came into the fellowship, most members trod lightly around the topic of spirituality. Compared to what we have become accustomed to, the attitudes of the founders seem almost old-fashioned. Of course, the main rationale for this policy now is that newcomers will be turned off if we focus too intently on the spiritual. But I wonder if we have not unwittingly lost something extremely important in our efforts to be urbane and nonthreatening. We will look at this issue more closely later, when we discuss the early days of the Steps.

However, what is important here is the early pioneers' primary focus on the undeniably spiritual nature of recovery. As we move on, we can find out how the founders availed themselves of some of the world's most sophisticated psychologies to validate and support their spiritual efforts.

WILLIAM JAMES—UNKNOWING FOUNDER

Do you remember in the previous chapter our discussion of Bill W.'s spiritual experience? We were wondering what to make of it—whether it was a hallucination or a true change of consciousness. It is interesting that, according to *Pass It On*, this is exactly the same sort of soul-searching Wilson himself went through right after the awakening. Fortunately, Bill received the encouragement of Dr. Silkworth. What a blessing to be validated by someone in the medical establishment! Silkworth's example could certainly stand as a blueprint for the future relationships between doctors and suffering addicts.

On the third day following the event, Ebby brought Bill a copy of James's *Varieties of Religious Experience*. From its description of the many types of spiritual awakenings found throughout the world, Bill was able to isolate three common dynamics: calamity, the admission of defeat, and the appeal to a Higher Power. Once again, can you recognize these concepts? Right here are the root principles of the first three Steps, which are themselves the foundation of the entire Twelve Step program.

We are told that Bill really needed support and validation for the shattering revelations he had encountered. He wanted to be sure he was not crazy. What he received from William James was the unquestioned backing of psychology itself. Haven't we been looking for the same thing as we seek to fathom the deeper mysteries of recovery? In returning to the roots of our practice, it is quite a surprise to find that our most provocative questions have long since been answered by the experiences of the founders themselves.

In summary, from a practical standpoint, William James helped Bill to see that a spiritual experience wasn't pathology. Thereafter, it could be documented as a valid, integral part of recovery's foundation. Bill had such admiration for the psychologist that later he was to refer to him as one of the founders of AA, even though James had been dead for many years.

CARL JUNG—SPIRITUS CONTRA SPIRITUM

Throughout his sobriety, Bill remembered what the famous European psychiatrist had told Roland. Jung told him that psychiatry could not heal an addict. The only thing that could help, he said, was a conversion experience, or a radical rearrangement of consciousness. This has certainly proven to be the truth of our experience, as well. In later years, Bill felt that it was necessary to thank Dr. Jung for his behind-the-scenes contribution to the founding of AA. So in 1961 he wrote a letter to him, expressing AA's indebtedness.

Jung responded by passing on two remarkable concepts, which have become powerful symbols of AA's spirituality. First, he said that the craving for alcohol was a low-level equivalent to the thirst of our being for wholeness. Jung's belief served to reinforce Bill W.'s own feeling, and those of many recovering persons, that alcohol provided a pseudospirituality that seemed to temporarily assuage the alcoholic's search for fulfillment.

The second principle was Jung's now-famous phrase, "spiritus contra spiritum." It is fascinating that the Latin word *spiritus* means both "spirit" and "spirits," or alcohol. Thus this Latin dictum means that spirituality is the only thing that can heal alcoholism.

If our addiction is what Jung believed it to be, a thirst for wholeness, then our recovery ought to include a way for us to experience this wholeness—not just a small part of it, but even wholeness itself. It's not that we all *must* search for wholeness. We are each guided by our own Higher Power to seek what attracts us. But if this is how we identify our search, then it is important to know that the Steps are more than up to the task of taking us there.

Couldn't it also be that the dis-ease we have been exploring is none other than this same thirst? And if this is so, shouldn't we do everything we can to honor the thirst, perhaps even devote ourselves to quenching it altogether?

The call within us to take this uncertain journey appears to have been sanctioned since the founding of the program. Bill W. and others heard the call and spent their lives answering it.

Already we can begin to see that the search is our right, and that, upon hearing the call, the only failure would be to deny that we have heard it.

The relationship between Carl Jung and the Twelve Steps is one of the most powerful talismans we can take with us as we journey beyond the crossroads. From the beginning of the Twelve Step movement, psychology and spirituality have been connected in a wonderful synergy whose full power is yet to be realized. And today many of us find ourselves willing to be a part of this flowering of the Steps. We have only to reach deep into the core of our path, bring forward this time-honored, living connection, and use it for what its purpose has always been—to quench the thirst for wholeness.

In the next chapter we will introduce some of the key guidelines from Jung's philosophy that can help us find our way into the new territory of the Steps. But there are other roots beneath the program we can draw strength from as well.

TAKING IT EASIER—FROM EXPERIENCE TO AWAKENING

The taproot of AA is the spiritual power that flowed through Bill W.'s radical experience. Upon this conversion experience, the 180-degree turnaround, rests the vision of the Steps that has evolved into the AA program. We place this truth above all others. It is essential that we do this, especially now, as we glean from our inheritance those newly revitalized principles which will become the inspiration for the next phase of our adventure.

I have always found it fascinating that Bill underwent his awakening before the Steps were ever written. This brings to mind the many source stories of the world's philosophical systems, in which so often the originators had just such a visionary experience in their beginnings. It seems that before creeds and dogmas are created, there is a revelation from which all future philosophy flows.

Although we recovery seekers express belief in the importance of the spiritual dimension in recovery, we become much more adept at practicing the medical and psychological disciplines than we do the spiritual. For whatever reason, we all too often treat the mystery of spirituality as a sacred cow. (We will look at this issue more closely in a later chapter.) It remains somehow untouchable and too mysterious for in-depth study.

The roots of this interesting form of spiritual denial were first manifested when Bill was writing the Steps. Originally, the term *God* was used instead of *Higher Power*. *Higher Power* was substituted so that atheists, agnostics, and all those who might have difficulties with anything sounding the least bit religious could feel less threatened. It was a brilliant decision. Without this kind of open-mindedness from the start, AA would have gone the way of the Oxford Group and countless other organizations that have been rendered irrelevant because of their dogmatism.

But even after the Big Book was written, AA's early members sought to further modify the essence of the spiritual message. They agreed to change the wording of the Twelfth Step from "having had a spiritual experience" to "having had a spiritual awakening." In initiating this change, they relied on distinctions that William James made between an experience, a "sudden upheaval," and an awakening, a gradual opening of the "educational variety."

I believe that this change was important and necessary, and that it had a lot to do with society's acceptance of AA. However, modifying the nature of the spiritual experience was much more of a double-edged sword than changing the word *God* to *Higher Power*, and had many more far-reaching, if subtle, consequences.

On the one hand, it certainly opened wide the doors of AA. But on the other, it unintentionally watered down the original emphasis on the power of spirituality in recovery. It was almost as though Bill's episode was more of a fluke. Over the years, most people have made the gradual awakening the focus of their practice. The original mysterious power, the sacredness, and the shattering change of consciousness itself that is the result of a radical experience are treated almost as a Twelve Step myth.

Later we will explore spirituality and how it has evolved to suit the times. But for our purposes here, it is sufficient to say that this subtle and gradual de-emphasizing of the spiritual component is one of the main reasons why so many of us are now at a loss to accept the emergence of spiritual power in our recovery. *The essence of recovery is spirituality.* The Steps were originally intended to help facilitate a spiritual experience. In general, we have used them to aid us in having a gradual awakening, and this is good. But we have not let them reveal to us their original intention of producing the radical dispensation that Bill received.

Bill W.'s recovery is our blueprint. He had both the *shattering* change of consciousness, even, as we said, before the Steps were written, and the *gradual* change that only working a program over many years, one day at a time, could produce. Why shouldn't we make room for both of these forms of change? They are both vital facets of the gift of recovery, and we owe it to ourselves to honor each of them on our own journey.

BILL W.—BEYOND THE CROSSROADS

One of the most exciting yet little-talked-about periods in Bill W.'s life was his experimentation with LSD. Although, for obvious reasons, it has been a subject of some controversy, this interesting interlude seems to have received official sanction when it was related at length in *Pass It On*.

This episode came much later in the evolution of AA than the other periods we have been discussing. Although it really had no direct bearing on the program's philosophical development, Bill's psychedelic exploration has particular relevance for those of us who are ourselves beginning to feel the call to explore.

But before we go further, we should preface our discussion with a few remarks concerning the potential controversy in adding a section on psychedelic use here. First and foremost, recovery is about *abstinence*. Including this discussion is *not* about taking substances; it is about examining Bill W.'s intentions when *he* took them. Then we can ascertain whether this type of curiosity can possibly be beneficial to us on our own adventure.

Bill underwent an LSD session after having met psychedelic pioneers Humphry Osmond and Abram Hoffer, who had already been doing clinical research with alcoholics and other addicts Bill W. wanted to see if this type of therapy could be used in the treatment of addiction. According to *Pass It On*, he had some very positive and uplifting experiences, which led him to believe that psychedelic work held bright promise for suffering addicts. He found that psychedelics helped facilitate a breaking through of ego defenses and alcoholic denial. Any method that could mediate a First Step experience, Bill felt, was of potential value in treatment.

In his own enthusiastic style, Bill shared his excitement with the fellowship. Not surprisingly, it was not reciprocated. After much debate, he was persuaded to tone down his endorsement of LSD and to keep his own private interests, however much they might help other alcoholics, separate from those of the fellowship. For those of us who have lived through the incredible spread of drug addiction that began a few years later, it's a good thing that Bill's friends intervened when they did.

But this in no way negates the value of this psychedelic work and its importance, both in Bill's own life and in the evolution of AA itself. What is meaningful is not that Bill took LSD, but that he demonstrated for all of us a vibrant, unswerving dedication to following wherever his Higher Power might lead, even if it went against the normally accepted standards of his contemporaries in the program. What is inspiring is that he remained ever the pioneer, and that he went through this crossroads in his own recovery. He was willing to venture into the unknown and to explore further horizons of the Steps, just as our own Higher Power is leading us to do.

If Bill were alive today, he would probably still not champion psychedelics publicly. But I believe he would be thrilled beyond his wildest dreams about the many powerful *nondrug* techniques available now that explore the same deeper dimensions of spirituality that he found LSD provided access to. However, these nondrug techniques *are* available to *us*. They are part of the "treasure trove" of methods that support Twelve Step practice. These are the Eleventh Step keys that open wide the doors on the broader domains of the Steps. Later, we will study these strategies to understand how they may prove useful as we seek to improve conscious contact with our Higher Power.

It is fitting to conclude this discussion of Bill W.'s consciousness research with a mention of his friendship with Aldous Huxley. Huxley, author of *The Doors of Perception* and *Brave New World*, is considered one of the preeminent philosophers of our time. He himself called Bill W. the greatest social architect of this century. This also demonstrates how Bill's admiration of philosophy and psychology was not a one-way street, but was in fact reciprocated by some of the great thinkers of the day. Once again, we discover a powerful interface between the Steps and philosophy.

These connections we have uncovered between the Steps and psychology and between the program and consciousness research provide us with incontrovertible evidence of the profound depth of the Twelve Step movement. Later we will unveil the crowning identification—the Twelve Step philosophy and world spiritual systems. Then we will have established the Steps as a classic world spiritual practice.

CONCLUSION—RADICAL RETURN TO ROOTS

The journey we are now taking is not an ungrounded departure from true Twelve Step practice. It is, in fact, a radical return to its philosophical roots and more accurately fulfills the original intentions of recovery pioneers. The path we now follow restores to our practice the original emphasis on spirituality as the founders understood it.

The Steps were designed to produce nothing less than spiritual experience. For whatever reason, many have lost touch with this early truth. And because of this, it has been an agonizingly lonely and frightening time for those of us who, through our own heartfelt willingness to surrender, are being led to rediscover what the founders always knew.

Real in-depth self-exploration, which inevitably leads to spiritual discovery, is threatening to many. Often we seem to be in the grip of a spiritual denial that is just as powerful as an addictive denial. It is time for us to accept the gifts of the founding members and use them for what they were intended—our own spiritual exploration. As we do this, we can hold up Bill W.'s own experience as a blueprint for our journey.

Radical ideas in our program do not, in and of themselves, require us to undergo major upheaval. AA itself was built on radical concepts. It has *always* been revolutionary. What is emerging for us now is the natural and inevitable outcome of working the Steps. Whatever made us think we could reach anything like complete understanding of this philosophy? Why shouldn't new and mysterious crossroads reveal themselves on our way?

I believe we go forward with the program's blessing. We have looked back one more time and have found what we were searching for. Thus it is almost time to leap. Our thirst for wholeness beckons us. The next chapter completes our outfitting for the journey by providing some maps to the territories we may be exploring.

CHAPTER FIVE

New Maps—The Wave and the Ocean

> *The whole drift of my education goes to persuade me that the world of our present consciousness is only one out of many worlds of consciousness that exist, and that those other worlds must contain experiences which have meaning for our life also; and that although in the main their experiences and those of this world keep discrete, yet the two become continuous at certain points, and higher energies filter in.*
>
> —William James

> *We have to find a life in the world of grace and the spirit, and this is certainly a new dimension for most of us.*
>
> —Bill W.

We are ready to begin final preparations for our adventure. At this point, the territory beyond the crossroads may feel completely unknown. But fortunately for us, many have been this way before. And of those who have made the journey, some have seen fit to chart their course, leaving maps for the rest of us who follow. Although maps are definitely *not* the territory, they can at least help make the unknown begin to feel known.

We have already touched upon how other cultures throughout history have made this journey beyond the crossroads an integral part of their societies. In a later chapter, we will see how their maps might be useful for us as we travel deeper into the Steps.

For now, however, we are more interested in how Western psychology has charted these regions. It is important to begin with a discipline with which we are already somewhat acquainted, and one that uses contemporary language. As we proceed, we will also define some of the terms that are frequently employed by the mapmakers. Later we can expand our horizons to include the contributions of other cultures. By then, we should be equipped with some practical information to add to the faith we have already been relying on.

We know that recovery is a matter of life and death. If we are facing the crossroads crisis we have described, then it is essential that we discover some new ways to bring the Steps to life. It would be so much easier if a second volume of the Big Book that described in detail this next recovery phase were suddenly published, thereby sanctioning our efforts once and for all.

But this will not happen. We must be content with the words of the only Big Book we have when it tells us, "More will be revealed." And this is exactly what is happening. More *is* being revealed right now to thousands of recovering persons. In a sense, the Higher Power is adding new chapters to the recovery story through each of us. We are being asked to answer the call of the Steps in a way uniquely our own, based solidly on the wealth of experience that has already come through traditional program practice.

We have made the decision to heed the call. It is gratifying to know that of those who have answered it before us, some have foreseen that we might be following them later. Therefore, in a spirit of gratitude, let's open some of the gifts they have given us.

THE PSYCHE

Are you familiar with the old "Star Trek" introduction, "Space—the final frontier . . ."? Well, despite the notion that space exploration is our greatest challenge, I believe the true final frontier is the journey we are now taking. This is the voyage, not outward, but within, into the infinite regions of what has come to be called our psyche. This is not a galaxy of physical planets. It is a dimension beyond the physical altogether, of which our bodies feel a part, a universe composed of what Carl Jung might call "memories, dreams, and reflections."

There is another deep connection between psychology and spirituality, which can be found in this root word, *psyche*. *Psyche* comes from the Greek, and has most often been employed to mean "mind." Consequently, when we think of psychology, we generally refer to the study of the mind. Certainly, this is the way traditional Western thinkers have envisioned it.

But in fact, a hidden, and perhaps truer, meaning of psyche is "soul"; and this connotation, apart from just the term *mind*, has far more relevance to us now. Although most of us have some powerful negative associations with words like *soul*, it is not too difficult to step back from the pull of these and take a more objective look at what the concept of *soul* implies. In the same way we were taught to envision our Higher Power, we can examine the term *soul* from a spiritual rather than a religious perspective.

In many philosophical systems, humans are seen as having a dual nature. One part of this nature is the soul, or higher self, which seems to be more directly connected to the Higher Power. The other part is a lower self, sometimes called the *ego*, which consists of patterns created by our character defects and is controlled by our addictions. Basically, these ideas do not conflict with the philosophy of the Big Book.

If we can let go of our old religious ideas, this concept of soul as the part of our being that is more connected to and guided by the Higher Power makes a lot of sense. But what *is* important is that *psyche*, the root word of *psychology*, originally implied something of a spiritual nature.

It is also interesting that traditional psychology has evolved to mean the study of the mind and has severed itself from the pursuit of spirituality. I believe that this is one of the main reasons why many of us are asking, Is this all there is? We are sensing that there is a missing piece in all the psychologies we have used as helpmates to our Twelve Step practice. To be true to its original meaning, psychology should be the study of the spiritual capacities of the mind, as well as its other more traditional functions. This is exactly what transpersonal psychology is now doing, as we pointed out earlier.

For our own purposes, we must arrive at a practical and functional definition of the psyche, yet one that also includes a spiritual component. Remember, our adventure is taking us *into* the psyche. It is about inner self-exploration. What we are looking for here are some maps to chart our expedition into the farther horizons of the psyche, where we feel the Steps may be leading us.

Freud said that the psyche was a *tabula rasa*, or a clean slate, at the time of birth. Each person has a psyche, and each person's psyche, or mind, is primarily bound and shaped by the events of early childhood.

For those of us who are feeling the call of our Higher Power, this understanding seems restrictive. The psyche feels infinitely larger than this. Our intuition tells us that it must include not just our own individual thoughts and feelings, but also all our spiritual aspirations, which seem to take us beyond the skin-encapsulated ego. We feel there must be a "fourth dimension" to the psyche, a realm of spirit underlying, or perhaps overshadowing, the impressions of what has happened to us in our lifetime.

So we will envision the psyche as it was originally intended—as soul, or spirit, as well as mind, a realm intimately connected with the Higher Power. And, as it includes spirit, we must also assume that it is a realm of great mystery, beyond anything traditional psychology has imagined.

CONSCIOUSNESS

Probably our most important connection with the term *consciousness* has been in our practice of the Eleventh Step, in which we are told to seek to improve "conscious contact" with the Higher Power by using the twin disciplines of prayer and meditation. Just what do we mean by "conscious contact?"

First of all, the simplest definition of being "conscious" is being "aware." Therefore, consciousness is awareness. So when we speak of "conscious contact," we are implying an experience of being aware of a connection with the Higher Power. Conscious contact means much more than just thinking about the Higher Power or desiring this connection. It literally means *having an experience*.

One of the tried and true axioms of psychotherapy is that we cannot be free of something until we are conscious of its existence.

It is possible, then, to say that healing, or becoming whole, is about becoming more conscious. We certainly can attest to this, as we recall our Fourth Step work. That entire process was about becoming aware, or conscious, of the circumstances of our past so that we could offer them up to our Higher Power through the further actions of the Steps, particularly the Sixth and Seventh.

A companion principle to the one above is that what we are unaware or unconscious of controls us. We well remember being a slave to our addiction, unconscious of what we were doing to ourselves and others. Our recovery began when we became conscious of our powerlessness. From this, we can see that there is a great power in consciousness itself. This does not mean that we are completely healed when we make something conscious. But it *does* mean that, with consciousness, the healing process has begun. This beginning should then be followed up with whatever other methods we may have at our disposal to further recovery.

Consciousness is an important concept for us to be familiar with for several reasons. First, most psychologies use the term *unconscious* to denote the part of the psyche that underlies our conscious waking self. It is seen as consisting of everything that has happened to us, what we can remember, and what we are no longer aware of. Each psychology has a particular strategy or strategies for getting in touch with unconscious material, just as we have used the Steps as our method.

What we are conscious of seems to set the boundaries of our growth. For example, the Sufis, a spiritual—not religious—branch of the Muslim faith, sometimes speak of consciousness from two perspectives. They call these the "worm's-eye" and the "eagle's-eye" views. Imagine the difference between these two. From the vantage point of the worm, life is limited to what is directly in front of it or underneath it. Time proceeds slowly, and the worm's experience is circumscribed by what little territory is covered.

But consider the eagle's-eye view. From this perspective, one has an all-encompassing vision of the big picture. The experience of time and space are drastically altered, and one can see clearly not only where one has been, but also where one is headed—the domain of the future—and what is compelling one to move forward.

We are not saying that one of these levels of consciousness is in itself better than the other. Both seem to have their value. It would be ideal if we were able to have access to each of them in our own lives. We ought to be able to live our lives as healthy individuals, taking care of the obligations directly in front of us. We ought to be able to move carefully, like the worm, yet also fly like the eagle to the mountaintop, as Bill W. did, and be conscious of the wind of spirit blowing through us.

This is where our own present search enters the picture. We have all explored the personal unconscious—what has happened to us since our birth—and we have uncovered many things. We have dealt with our childhood traumas and what we feel are the origins of our codependence and shame. Yet we still feel incomplete. Thus we find ourselves at the crossroads, looking for new strategies to access our unconscious, and, more than that, looking for new maps and definitions of what the psyche and the unconscious actually are.

Ultimately, we discover new meanings for the term *consciousness* itself. We begin to see that consciousness research denotes far more than just taking LSD and engaging in practices that do not seem to have any real relevance for us in our recovery. We come to understand that this research is a modern Western approach for the time-honored practice of self-exploration. It is an examination of the many wonderful ways seekers have for all time pursued this objective.

Finally, it is possible to begin to see consciousness in a whole new light, beyond the restrictions placed upon it by traditional schools of psychology. If we study the world's philosophies, we can observe how many have given consciousness expansion the highest priority. They have even gone so far as to say that we ourselves *are* consciousness. Furthermore, if we use any of the many time-honored approaches, we can have this experience as well. We can experience the fourth dimension. We can feel an ever-expanding conscious contact with our Higher Power, even to the point of experiencing ourselves as an actual part of this power and of all creation.

All these experiences, we are told, can be ours—and many more. They are an unspoken part of the Promises. Our purpose is to utilize the Steps and continue to expand our consciousness. We already know what this feels like. Coming into the program was a tremendous expansion of consciousness for us. Reaching out to the fellowship made us aware of other human beings in a new way. Our feelings are no longer restricted to painful emotions, and our thought life has been freed from the chains of obsession.

Isn't this consciousness expansion? Isn't our practice of the Steps the same thing as consciousness research? It is not too difficult a leap of faith to see that the exploration we are preparing to do is the logical extension of the search we have already been on. It is just that now, as we are becoming conscious of farther horizons, we see that our understanding of the psyche and of spirituality must expand to keep pace. So let us continue and find out how other voyagers before us have charted their discoveries.

THE MAVERICKS

Carl Jung

Of his many students in the psychoanalytical movement, Sigmund Freud considered Carl Jung one of the most promising. But as frequently happens, the student split from the teacher and became influential in his own right. Jung felt that Freud's interpretations and maps of the psyche were too restrictive to account for the incredibly vast array of experiences available to humans.

Jung believed that the Freudian perspective—that the human psyche consists only of experiences from the personal history or biography—was incomplete. The model broke down when it attempted to categorize experiences of a spiritual or nonpersonal nature by reducing them to the level of the personality. Jung felt that the personal history was just the tip of the iceberg and that there were other dimensions of the psyche that influenced the psychological and spiritual lives of seekers. He called this further dimension the *collective unconscious*.

We have already mentioned the collective in our chapter on new ideas. At that juncture, we compared it to a principle of modern physics. We said that the psyche has a particle, or individual nature, as well as a wave, or collective nature, much in the same way that light has dual characteristics. We went on to point out that in order to recover fully, we must get in touch with, or make conscious, both these aspects of our being.

According to Jung, the collective unconscious is a dimension of consciousness that is common to all humanity. It is like a vast reservoir of material that seems to surround or interpenetrate the psyches of individuals. Jung felt that not only could we have the experience of being *a* human, but we could also experience ourselves as *humanity* itself.

One of the most important of Jung's contributions was to include spirituality in the domain of the collective psyche, not as pathology, but as an integral part of a human being's quest. He felt that the spiritual impulse was a more driving force of the psyche, more powerful, even, than sexuality, which Freud considered to be the primary motivating dynamic. In fact, Jung believed that the sex drive, or libido, was actually part of a much larger and more compelling creative force that was essentially spiritual.

Joseph Campbell, one of the great philosophers and mythologists of our time, used to say that Freud was fishing while sitting on a whale. Although his contribution has been immense, it seems that Freud barely scratched the surface of human potential. What he believed to be the entire range of experiences possible to humans turns out to be, upon further exploration, only the *foam* on the surface of a *wave*, on the surface of an *ocean* of consciousness.

Within this ocean, the collective dimension, are vast psychological and spiritual forces that influence our personality and the way we live, just as there are events in our childhood that combine to mold our future. Jung called these dynamics *archetypes*. Basically, an archetype is an original blueprint, or a model, from which all future examples of something are derived.

Jung believed that archetypes exist within the psyche, independently of individuals, as core patterns that help shape and give meaning to the individual personality. They are not merely symbolic of dynamics in the biography, but are distinct structures in their own right whose existence is derived from another dimension of the psyche.

Jung's concept of archetypes was not a total departure from traditional Western philosophy, but in fact had its roots in what many consider to be the wellspring of Western thought. Archetypes are very similar to Plato's concept of Ideas. Although students of philosophy have pointed to differences between these two, it is validating that this seemingly revolutionary principle is grounded solidly in Greek thought and, hence, the fabric of the Western mind.

Here is a layperson's explanation, which helps to clarify what archetypes are and how they influence our recovery. You will have to use your imagination, but we have already been told in the Twelve and Twelve that "constructive imagination" is a vital life tool. Picture, if you can, that within the collective dimension of the psyche, there is the archetype of the Human Being. This blueprint contains every conceivable possibility of human traits—physical, mental, emotional, and spiritual. We could say that the archetypal Human exists within us as a pure potential waiting to manifest.

Every individual human being is a representative of this archetype in the world. According to a creative process, which we imagine can exist only within the realm of the Higher Power, we each manifest certain characteristics of this one Human. In a sense, we are participating in "humanness." Every possible form of humanness is somehow available to us. And each characteristic is itself an archetype, from which our own particular demonstration of the blueprint is derived.

For example, if a mother feels love for her child, her love is a manifestation of the archetype of Motherhood. Then, according to this school of thought, she can experience not only this quality of *individual* love, but also what it feels like to be, in a sense, *every* mother, with a universal love for *all* children. Can you see from this how we grow into connectedness? To be not only a mother but somehow *the* mother is a richer, fuller experience that transcends separateness and individuality. It is a way to move beyond fragmentation into wholeness.

Not only can she begin to experience the archetype of

Motherhood here, but she can also connect with the archetype of Love, of which love of a mother for a child is only one of many aspects. There is also romantic love and the love of a seeker for the Higher Power or some cause or ideal, as well as many other forms. What makes this so fascinating is that the blueprint of Motherhood exists within the collective psyche of *everyone*, not just mothers. Everyone—men, children, and women who have not been mothers—can all truly know, from the inside, what it feels like to be a mother.

This is the importance of our experiencing archetypes in recovery. Many have said that addiction is a sickness of isolation and that recovery is about becoming a part of something larger than the separate self. To be able to experience—not just think about or imagine, but actually *experience*—within ourselves other facets of humanity is the surest way to transcend our sense of isolation. To begin to connect with the archetypes underlying our individual selves by the action of our Higher Power working through the Steps represents a further horizon of recovery. It opens the door on a vast realm of collective experiences, which can help free us from the restrictions of separateness. We will then be able to see not only that we are an *individual* part of humanity, but also that we have access to the *whole* of humanity and even the cosmos itself.

AA is no stranger to archetypes. In a very real sense, the Higher Power is itself an archetype. Within the concept of the Higher Power exists every thought, feeling, or experience anyone could ever have about that Power. We might discover for ourselves any one of an infinite number of understandings of God, the group, or even religion. It appears that a particular constellation of characteristics of this Higher Power archetype are manifested through each of us. And somehow our Higher Power directs us to ever-expanding definitions of Its own mysterious nature. And the Higher Power is always greater than any definition or concept we may have about It.

The Broad Highway is another beautiful example of an archetype, and one that is so close to home too. We can now begin to envision just how wide this Broad Highway may actually be. By now we can surely see that not only are all recovering persons traveling it, but also that seekers of all kinds everywhere have journeyed on it as well. What's more, our eyes are now opening to more new distances in the unfolding of the Highway than we ever knew existed.

We know already that Bill expressed his indebtedness to Jung because he felt that the Jungian perspective was so influential to AA's foundation. But I believe that Jung's most profound contribution is only now being revealed. As the Higher Power begins to show us the vast and ageless dimensions of the psyche, we can truly feel grateful to be a part of recovery's new horizon.

Roberto Assagioli

Roberto Assagioli was a contemporary of Carl Jung and, like Jung, a rebellious disciple of Freud. Assagioli also believed that there were further dimensions to the psyche beyond the personal biography. He was the founder of psychosynthesis, a method of human growth based on integrating the many different aspects of humanness into one harmonious whole.

Assagioli advocated strongly that the spiritual and collective dimensions of the psyche must be included in any true model of psychological health. In developing psychosynthesis, he drew upon many sources, from Freudian psychoanalysis and the Jungian perspective to Eastern mysticism and mystical Christianity.

He, too, developed an extended map of the psyche, which includes, but goes further than, the personality self. His model is quite detailed, but it basically consists of a lower self, or the personality or "ego" self; and a higher, or "transpersonal" self, which is a part of the superconscious, or spiritual dimension. There is also an unconscious realm, which he divided into the lower, middle, and higher unconscious. According to Assagioli, the directing principle in the system is the "self," which uses the action of the will. The self is connected to, and actually part of, the Universal Self, which is sometimes called the All, or the One. In our terminology, this would be the part of us connected to the Higher Power.

The actual therapeutic process of psychosynthesis is divided into several stages. The first is becoming conscious of the hidden material. These uncovered patterns Assagioli called *subpersonalities*, some of which are similar to what we call character defects. The second part concerns itself with acceptance of and surrender to the existence of the subpersonalities. The third part is disidentifying with them, or letting them go. The final stage is about integration and synthesis, or developing the consciousness of a new self, which has become aware of its identification with the higher self, or its connection to the Higher Power. Again, it is easy to see the similarities between psychosynthesis and the actions of the Twelve Steps.

Like Abraham Maslow, whose work we have mentioned, Assagioli believed that spirituality was a sign of health, not pathology. His philosophy was centered on the inherent goodness of the individual, as opposed to the basic Freudian perspective, which essentially concerned itself with what was wrong with human beings psychologically.

Carl Jung and Roberto Assagioli were not the only renegades of their time to question the assumptions of traditional psychology. However, it is important to highlight these two in particular for two reasons: first, they each spearheaded vital movements in the evolution of psychology, and second, they both formulated expanded maps of the human psyche that include the spiritual dimension. Many recovering persons today have used these models as helpmates in their own practice.

We can say that these pioneers are the forerunners of today's transpersonal psychology—the West's contemporary discipline that includes the contributions of the entire field of psychology, as well as the gifts from what Aldous Huxley has called the "perennial philosophy." It is time to explore what the nineties have to offer us in the way of modern maps. We can then ascertain for ourselves whether some current cartography might prove to be the ideal helpmate for us on our journey.

THE NEW SCHOOL

There is an interesting anecdote from the famous modern psychiatrist and consciousness researcher Stanislav Grof about the beginnings of transpersonal psychology. He was discussing his first meetings with Abraham Maslow, Viktor Frankl, Jim Fadiman, Anthony Sutich, and others, during which they founded psychology's latest force.

Each of these pioneers had been working independently of the others, using different methods, but were coming up with the same results. Their findings all pointed to the fact that healing seemed to happen when seekers gained access to further reaches of the psyche, or when they came into conscious contact with some form of spirituality.

Grof dryly observed that when you are out there all alone and you come up with some radical new ideas, you are considered a maverick. But when a group of these solitary renegades gets together, then you have a school.

This is one humorous angle on the birth of transpersonal psychology. From another point of view, transpersonal psychology is the natural outcome of a number of things: First, it is part of the evolution of Western psychology itself—from Freud through the mavericks Jung, Assagioli, Reich, Rank, and others; to Maslow and beyond. Second, it is the flowering of the consciousness research movement, as exemplified by Stanislav Grof, Humphrey Osmond, Richard Alpert, Jim Fadiman, and others. Third, it reveals itself to be a modern Western discipline synthesizing psychology and the great spiritual traditions of the world. And finally, as we have already shown in chapter 3, "New Ideas," it represents an attempt at reconciling the disparities between psychology, spirituality, and science, creating a synergy never before accomplished in the history of the West.

We have already discussed the ground-breaking work of Abraham Maslow and his study of the "peak experience." We did not, however, mention his concepts of "meta-values" and "meta-motivations." Maslow believed that these represented further dimensions of human potential that went beyond just the individual personality and onward to include spiritual realities. In a sense, this research can also be called an extended map of the psyche. It is probably safe to say that Maslow can be considered the father of transpersonal psychology, as well as the father of humanistic psychology.

One of the great mapmakers of the transpersonal movement is

Ken Wilber. In a series of complex and challenging books, he has succeeded in bringing together in one system the entire spectrum of Western psychology and the major principles of the best known of the world's spiritual disciplines. Again, even a basic outline of his work is too large a task for this book. For the earnest seeker who enjoys a conceptual workout, we have provided a list of this amazing theoretician's contributions in the Bibliography.

However, I believe it is extremely important in our undertaking to include the extended cartography of Stanislav Grof. For over a decade his map has been used by thousands of seekers, including recovering persons, in their adventures beyond the crossroads. Let's examine his system and see what components in its structure make it so accessible to modern-day journeyers.

GROF'S "REALMS OF THE HUMAN UNCONSCIOUS"

Over many years Stanislav Grof compiled the experience of thousands of seekers who had journeyed into the realms of the psyche using a variety of strategies—everything from traditional psychological techniques to psychedelics, meditation, drumming, and breathwork. Then he organized the data into categories, based on the mental, emotional, and spiritual characteristics of the experiences. As a result, he found that all of them fell within four distinct realms, which he called "bands" of consciousness.

These bands, or levels, of consciousness make up Grof's extended cartography of the psyche. What is exciting about his map is that he never says that this is *what* the psyche is. He only says that based on the reports of seekers, this is *one* way to envision the multiple realms of the unconscious. It is easy to trust this type of approach, because it does not ask us to accept some radical, unprovable theory as the truth. There seems to be more of an "Isn't this interesting" or "See for yourself" attitude about the material.

Over the years, Grof has advocated the use of powerful methods to access the various levels of the psyche. These techniques have been employed by thousands of seekers in their own journeys toward wholeness. Moreover, some of them are beginning to be used in addictions and mental health settings. In later chapters, we will examine these as part of the treasure trove of Eleventh Step tools. But without further introduction, let's take a look at the four levels.

The Sensory Level

One of the most common experiences in deep self-exploration seems to be an expanded sensory awareness. Hearing, inner vision, taste, touch, and smell all feel intensified. What seems to be happening is a cleansing of the "doors of perception," a term coined by the poet William Blake and later used by Aldous Huxley.

At the sensory level, there is no specific psychological content. In fact, this dimension seems to act as a barrier to deeper journeying, perhaps somehow prohibiting seekers from confronting something for which they are not prepared. We are reminded, at this point, of the well-known saying "Our Higher Power will not give us anything we cannot handle." It's comforting to know that this axiom will hold true when we venture beyond the boundaries of our own personal unconscious.

The Biographical Level

This is the dimension with which we are most familiar. Just as a "biography" is the story of someone's life, the biographical level is, according to Grof, everything that has happened in our lives since birth. We have all done biographical work, either with the Steps or with some form of psychology as helpmate. Fourth Step work deals with biographical material, as does family-of-origin work.

One further observation should be mentioned here. Grof found that in addition to the wide range of psychological material that one expects would emerge, a whole different set of experiences also surfaces. These are all the traumas that actually threaten the life of the seeker—illnesses, accidents, and near-death experiences. Since we ourselves are well aware of what it feels like to be in a life-threatening situation through our addiction, this information begins to sound intriguing.

The Perinatal Level

If this system was beginning to sound interesting before, there should be no doubt about it from this point on. The perinatal level quickly leaves the domain of the traditional and rockets us into a fourth dimension in its own right.

The word *perinatal* comes from the Greek and the Latin and means "of, or surrounding, birth." According to Grof, within this dimension are recorded all our experiences of the surrender process, or what the world traditions call "death and rebirth." It is also the level where we store the memory of our actual biological birth.

At first glance, this is a radical concept, and, given the traditional scientific and psychological framework we grew up with, one that is pretty hard to swallow. But the latest medical and psychological findings are beginning to see things differently. There have already been several conferences on perinatal psychology, presenting research on how we retain a record of our biological birth.

The research also shows that the birth experience can have a tremendous impact on our lives from the very beginning. Furthermore, undergoing deep self-exploration and making the birth experience conscious can greatly enhance the more traditional biographical work we may be doing. There is also fascinating evidence demonstrating that certain aspects of the birth can be a factor in addiction. This is something we will definitely want to explore later.

Grof sees the perinatal acting as an interface, or a dimension-doorway, between our personal, or particle, self and our transpersonal, or wave, self. The key, in light of our own adventure, is that the perinatal concerns itself with what we call the "First Step experience"—powerlessness and surrender—and death/rebirth. Can you begin to see the relevance of this map for deeper Twelve Step work?

The Transpersonal Level

Essentially, Grof sees the transpersonal dimension as coinciding with the collective unconscious. In this band are the archetypes and experiences of the world's mythologies, as well as a wide variety of spiritual experiences as they have been reported by different schools.

Many seekers who have entered the transpersonal are able to report that they let go of their exclusive identification with the body and the ego, and can have the consciousness of being any part of nature—animals, plants, rocks—or any part of the material universe. They also report experiencing what seem to be past lives, and a host of other phenomena. If the personal self can be experienced as a *limited* field of consciousness, then the transpersonal self can be seen as an *unlimited* field of awareness, or essentially "all that is."

Grof does not join the debate over whether reincarnation or some of these other seemingly outrageous phenomena are real or true, and neither will we. But what is important is that seekers' *experiences* of them are *definitely* real. And, what's more, they have repeatedly proven to be healing and an enhancement of recovery.

This is a modern map large enough to include any experience we might have, yet, more importantly, it is open-ended enough not to pigeonhole our process. Perennial wisdom says that the psyche is infinite. No reputable map could profess to have accurately charted it all. In a sense, Grof extends an invitation to the seeker to use the map, if it feels appropriate. And as we undertake what he calls the "adventure of self-discovery," we may just discover that we ourselves have become mapmakers in our own right.

WHY ARE WE HERE?—SOME CONCLUSIONS

Let's take stock of where we are so far in our study of the maps. How and why is this important to us? We all know that in order to maintain recovery, we must continue to use the Steps, and possibly psychology, to explore the domain of our past. But now we are discovering that the past is not quite what we thought it was. What we thought were the causes of our troubles turn out to be only partially, or relatively, causal.

Our past reveals itself to be much deeper than we ever imagined. It seems to recede and to expand ultimately into the far reaches of what we can only call a mystery. And equipped with our newfound information, we can see how the Mystery is itself an archetype, or attribute, of our Higher Power. This deep past also contains other levels of causality. Now we know that this recovery journey includes discovering and exploring these other dimensions of our psyche too.

Other intriguing insights are beginning to emerge for us as well. Our intuition tells us that we are not just driven forward by the events of our personal, or even transpersonal, past. Somehow, we are being *summoned* by a distant call, either from the future or from beyond time altogether. And what calls us seems to contain a blueprint of our wholeness. In short, we are guided by a Higher Power, almost as though it were a beacon far down the road in front of us.

When we choose to take on an Eleventh Step method, one of the safe, nondrug techniques that we are going to explore in the next chapter, vast forces of the psyche become mobilized and begin to emerge into our consciousness to be healed. As we said earlier, sometimes this emergence may feel painful. But it is a sign that we are doing it right, and that we are being led by the Steps.

Most of the time, a veil seems to separate our personal, everyday consciousness from our transpersonal nature. We are usually aware of being a separate individual and, for the most part, are unaware, at the level of actual experience, of our true identity with other humans or humanity itself. For some of us, the veil is quite thin, but for the majority of us, it is thick and seems almost impenetrable.

How does this veil part? Sometimes it parts naturally, of its own accord. It opens when we dream, when we are watching a beautiful sunset, or listening to some inspiring classical music or great rock and roll. It parts with an experience of great joy or great pain—in childbirth, in accidents, and in near-death experiences.

There are many methods specifically designed to lift the veil. Every culture throughout history has used them. Meditation parts the veil. Psychedelics, dancing, shamanic drumming, singing, and breathwork all part the veil. And we have definitely sought to lift it, too, through our addiction, somehow mistaking the temporary satiation of our craving for the true fulfillment that the call to go home is promising us. Yes, and the Twelve

Steps part the veil, as well. Bill W. and the pioneers knew this. If we look carefully, we can see how they also told us so, in the many poetic metaphors scattered throughout the texts.

Mythology, an integral part of the collective unconscious, beckons us to look at our childhood fairy tales once again. Recovery puts them in a new light and reanimates them. They can become personal testaments to the power of addiction and recovery, if we can read between the lines.

Do you remember the Greek myth of Icarus, who flew on wings made by his father to escape King Minos? In celebration of what he thought was his personal freedom, he ignored the warnings of his parent and flew so close to the sun that his wings melted. How like an addict! Icarus' crash to earth is so much like our own initial elation and ultimate disillusionment and destruction at the hands of our addiction.

And what of the story of Prometheus, who stole fire from the gods and was condemned to be chained to a rock and to have his liver devoured every day by a vulture? Every day, he raged at being bound. Each day the vulture came and tortured him. And each time his liver would grow back. Day after day, he raged, but the vulture always returned. What a metaphor for powerlessness and the seemingly endless nature of our own rage and torment!

These stories and hundreds like them are not just entertaining tales. They are experiences we can have from the collective psyche. They are examples of how other cultures have undergone the same great life crises that we must face. And for us to experience these challenges in the context of how other cultures have confronted them frees us from the narrow confines of our own small picture and connects us with humanity in a way that is ultimately "happy, joyous, and free."

We can also begin to see that there are transpersonal levels of the emotions we have always thought were personal. For example, the shame we know so well from our childhood, which we have sought to give back to our parents, turns out to be a universal feeling shared by humanity at large. What do we think our parents are supposed to do with it when we give it back to them? Should they give it to *their* parents, and they to theirs? In deep work we can experience shame, certainly as a trauma of our childhood, but also as something more than that. We may be able to see how it is part of our birth process, or perhaps how it is an integral piece of the human experience altogether. We can then become fully conscious of it, in all its ramifications, and ultimately "give it *all the way* back" to the Higher Power.

The same process holds true for aloneness. What we thought was a feeling caused primarily by childhood trauma reveals itself to have a transpersonal level too. We can actually have the experience of what it is like to leave the safety and unity of the Mother/Father God and be born as a separate individual. Or we can even reexperience what it was like to leave the connectedness of the womb and begin the torturous journey of physical birth.

It is also possible to make conscious a healing dimension of aloneness, such as the empowered nature of the warrior or the individual seeker, who stands apart, leaning on no one. We may discover these meanings and others wholly new to us, ones shared by all humanity.

There are collective dimensions to the positive emotions of our recovery as well. Certainly, coming into the program gave many of us our first real feeling of belonging. It is hard to imagine that there could be other, more expanded levels to connectedness. Yet this is what we discover as we work the Eleventh Step, ever improving our conscious contact, feeling more and more connected to the Higher Power than we ever could have imagined.

There were times when we felt that to be relieved of the obsessions and the compulsions of our addiction was the only freedom we need ever know. Although in a sense this is still true, we are truly grateful for the glimpses we have had of what it means to be free in other ways—of our own sense of separation, and even free from some of our character defects. Freedom itself becomes another archetype, one with many facets, and one which we can explore and experience ever-widening dimensions of.

It seems that all these positive emotions are like the horizon line—the more we travel toward them, the more any real sense of grasping them recedes. Our experience of them does not seem to have any boundaries. And if we follow where our Higher

Power leads, we can perhaps feel ourselves grow toward some archetype of the Self that only the Higher Power knows the limit of.

In taking a quick inventory, we can see that we have been validated and supported, and that our adventure is sanctioned by both the program and psychology. We have been given some practical guidelines and some very sophisticated maps to the territory we may be exploring.

But the one thing we do not yet have is a strategy, an actual way to part the veil. We have mentioned something called Eleventh Step methods. These will be the vehicles that will take us down the Broad Highway of the psyche. It is time now to examine a whole spectrum of these strategies so that we can choose the ones that feel most right for us as we embark.

CHAPTER SIX

The Treasure Trove—Eleventh Step Doorways

One should acquire practical knowledge of the Path by treading it.

—The Supreme Path (Tibetan)

The other Steps can keep us sober and somehow functioning. But Step Eleven can keep us growing, if we try hard and work at it continually.

—Bill W.

I am one of those for whom reading has always been inspirational. Even years before recovery, and always during it, I would steep myself in the words of the world's spiritual and psychological teachers. I found the many ways that seekers sought transformation fascinating, and it gave me hope that one day I could discover for myself the realms they described.

Along the way, however, I began to notice an interesting phenomenon. I realized that while I was reading about spirituality I felt really inspired. But in between books I would lapse back into emptiness, frustration, and longing. As soon as I would begin another text, though, the good feeling would come back, and everything seemed okay again. Somehow, reading *about* transformation, about surrender and death/rebirth, lulled me into believing that this actually equaled *experiencing* these dimensions.

After years of hopping from one book to the next, trying to maintain that spiritual buzz, it began to dawn on me that I was fooling myself. I finally realized that one of these days I was going to have to actually *do* some of the things that I had read about in all those books. This thought was a frightening revelation.

I saw, for example, that I could read every book ever written about swimming. I could memorize the techniques, the names of all the muscles used, and even the molecular composition of water. But none of these added up to the *experience* of swimming. At some point, I was going to have to *get in the water*.

In a sense, this is where we are in our own exploration. It is important that we have studied what others have had to say about the journey into spirituality. It has helped us shift our worldview, as well as provided us with much-needed hope and inspiration. Learning by reading is certainly an integral part of preparation.

But do you remember when you reached that stage in your Twelve Step practice when you were told that it was time for action? This is exactly where we are now. However, in order to act, we will need to use the techniques of action. We know that there is a treasure trove of methods available to us. I often think of it as a banquet table spread out before us, upon which are arrayed the gifts of the ages.

There are literally hundreds of psychological and spiritual practices available to us today. To explore even a fraction of these would be the task of many volumes. However, we can discuss a few that will, we hope, provide a cross-section of the entire spectrum. Then, with this basic overview of the banquet table, we should be better able to make an informed choice about which methods are right for us.

FAMILIAR TERRITORY

Let's start with some work that is probably familiar. Many of us either have been through treatment or have experienced some form of therapy as adjuncts to our recovery. We may be surprised to learn that some transpersonal strategies are already an integral part of many therapeutic plans.

Probably the most common is guided imagery, or creative visualization. We already have a precedent for this approach within the roots of the Twelve Step program. In the chapter on the Eleventh Step in the Twelve and Twelve, we are told that constructive imagination is an important part of a rewarding life. The section even uses a form of creative visualization, asking the reader to imagine being on a sunlit beach, contemplating spiritual realities.

My first experience with guided imagery was at a training seminar at the Johnson Institute in the early eighties. It was the first time that I was able to get in touch with my "inner child," and it initiated much of my family-of-origin work. For most of the eighties, creative visualization was used by many addictions therapists. It has been an important tool in helping seekers get in touch with early childhood trauma, as well as the Higher Power.

We mention this strategy here because they are many seekers' first exposure to doing work in non-ordinary states of consciousness. By *non-ordinary*, we mean that practitioners can dis-identify with just the ordinary everyday consciousness of being the body and the ego. By using the imagination, our consciousness frees itself from its exclusive identification with the body or the ego and seems to tap a creative dimension within us that is connected somehow to the Higher Power.

This is a form of consciousness expansion, as we discussed in the past chapter. During a guided imagery experience focusing on, for example, the inner child, we are our present self, but, in a sense, we are also the child. This is the paradox we described when we were discussing the emergence of a new paradigm that requires us to think in terms of "both/and" instead of "either/or."

THE JUNGIAN GIFTS

There are many books, teachers, and therapists with a Jungian perspective to choose from in the search to find approaches that are compatible with our program practice. However, two teachers come quickly to mind because they have focused specifically on addiction and recovery as part of their work.

The first of these is Marion Woodman. Her book *The Owl Was a Baker's Daughter* treats eating disorders from an archetypal perspective. She has also written two books dealing specifically with transformation of the modern woman: *The Pregnant Virgin* and *Addiction to Perfection*. Her work *The Ravaged Bridegroom* brings the archetypal approach to bear on transformational issues important to men.

Author and therapist Linda Leonard also deserves to be mentioned for her work bringing together recovery, the spiritual quest, and a Jungian orientation. Of her three books, *On the Way to the Wedding*, *The Wounded Woman*, and *Witness to the Fire*, the latter uses fairy tales and examples from world literature to explore the deeper roots of addiction and recovery.

One of the principal techniques of exploration in Jungian psychology is the analysis of dreams. From this perspective, dreams are seen as emergences from the unconscious—not just from the personal biography, but also from the collective, archetypal dimension. As the material surfaces into consciousness through dreams, it then has the potential for healing.

Have you ever had a dream during your recovery where you were engaged in active addiction again? There are many ways to interpret this. I think that the most restrictive viewpoint is to assume that it means we are doing it wrong or are in danger of relapsing. Although this may be true, there are other ways to perceive it.

Instead of being a sign of sickness, the drinking dream might be a sign of health. It could be a way that the Higher Power is healing us at a deeper level. The emergence of this type of material into consciousness during sleep could be signaling a clearing of hidden patterns in the unconscious, to which we could not have access in our waking state.

When I am having a dream like this, sometimes I wake up, still in the dream state, and remember that I am in recovery. Then it becomes a nightmare, and I experience tremendous anguish and remorse, just as if I had actually relapsed. Might it not be that this experience is a gift from the Higher Power, through the unconscious, allowing me to have a firsthand experience of what it used to be like? If I can have this experience in the non-ordinary state of a dream, I might not have to experience it in my waking life. In this sense, the dream is a healing gift.

PSYCHOSYNTHESIS

In the last chapter, we outlined the main principles of psychosynthesis and made some connections between them and the Twelve Steps. Many recovering persons have found this system to be a logical extension of their program. Since psychosynthesis uses a variety of experiential strategies, from guided imagery to dreamwork and different forms of meditation, it is difficult to pin it down.

However, we *can* mention a few concepts that can convey the essential value of this approach to recovery practice. A very good basic outline of psychosynthesis is found in Molly Young Brown's *The Unfolding Self*. We have already compared what we call character defects to what psychosynthesis refers to as subpersonalities. Although these concepts are similar, there are some important differences, especially in the attitude with which each is viewed by the practitioner.

In general, we in Twelve Step practice see character defects in a negative light. In fact, we often give them the religious connotation of "sins." Because these defects underlie our addictive behavior, we tend to put a moral judgment on them, even when we are trying to let go of some of our old religious programming. However, psychosynthesis practitioners see subpersonalities from an entirely different perspective.

Did you ever hear the true story of the Japanese soldier who was finally found on a South Seas island about twenty years after World War II? It seems he never knew that the fighting was over, so for all those years he behaved as if he were still at war. In *The Unfolding Self*, Brown makes a wonderful comparison between the soldier's actions and the way subpersonalities persistently hang on in our lives.

Brown says that these subpersonalities originally performed some constructive duties for us. We created them and used them for either emotional, physical, and spiritual survival during our times of trauma, or as healthy defenses to protect us when we really needed them. They are like loyal soldiers who have fought for us when no one outside us could.

The problem is that these soldiers are *extremely* loyal, and, just like the Japanese soldier, they do not know when the war is over or when to quit fighting. Now that we are older and are capable of developing new, less defensive life strategies, these mechanisms hang on and continue to operate in our lives. But now they have outlived their usefulness and only create more problems for us. They prevent us from developing healthy relationships and otherwise being at peace with ourselves.

Instead of putting a moral judgment on them and attacking them as though they were some form of sickness, Brown says that we should honor them for what they have done for us constructively. Instead of "going to war" against them all over again, we can somehow embrace them, learn from them, and accept them in all their characteristics. Then we can use our spiritual resources to begin to let them go.

This is a far cry from treating ourselves as though we were "bad" or "sinful," or as though our character defects needed to be cut out like a cancer. If we can remember what we learned in chapter 2, "Good News," we can even begin to see our character defects as at least partly the result of doing it right at one point in our lives. This is one of the most important contributions of psychosynthesis to Twelve Step practice. We can start viewing addiction and codependence from a wellness perspective, not just in terms of a disease model. In addition to Molly Young Brown's work, many seekers report that Piero Ferrucci's *What We May Be* is another accessible introduction to psychosynthesis.

OTHER TREASURES FROM THERAPY

Before we move on to our discussion of spiritual disciplines, there are other therapeutic techniques that we should mention. Among these are creative arts and other expressive therapies.

Many of the world's spiritual disciplines consider the creative urge and the spiritual impulse one and the same. There are also countless stories of how active addiction and codependence have been most destructive in the ways they have contributed to the stifling of these urges. In one sense, recovery can be seen as a gradual awakening of the creative drive within us.

Seekers report that awakening to creativity is like truly coming alive. Many more admit that they experience their most vital conscious contact with the Higher Power when they are painting, singing, dancing, or whatever. Still others say that when they were able to unblock the creative energies within themselves, they actually began to feel joy for the first time.

Michelle Cassou is an artist and teacher who helps seekers discover their creative potential in nontraditional ways. She believes that we are all artists. Her workshops are a joyful exercise in creativity at play. In addition to Cassou's method, there are many types of expressive therapies available that can help us tap the creative potential within us. Silvano Arieti's book *Creativity: The Magic Synthesis* offers a good overview for seekers hoping to tap the creative powers within. But let us not forget that we do not need a therapist to express ourselves. Again, we can let our intuition guide us in discovering which forms of creativity and play are best for us.

SHAMANISM

Shamanism is considered the oldest form of spirituality on the planet, dating back at least forty thousand years. Thanks to anthropologists and consciousness researchers who have studied and experienced its techniques, shamanic practices are now becoming available to us in the West as important psychological and spiritual tools.

Often called medicine women or men, shamans are individuals who have undergone many experiences in the further realms of the psyche. Because of their familiarity with these territories, they become effective guides for others who are less acquainted with the collective realms. Before they become recognized by their tribe or society as genuine healers, shamans usually must undergo a powerful experience that intimately identifies them with the realms of human suffering and subsequent transformation. Through these experiences, they become acquainted with surrender, death/rebirth, and the dynamics of personal and spiritual power.

This episode is sometimes called a shamanic crisis, or illness.

If we examine for a moment the nature of addiction and recovery, we can make a striking parallel between our disease and the shamanic crisis. Just as shamans use their illnesses or crises as a gift to guide others in their societies, recovering addicts and codependents are best able to carry the message to other sufferers. It is the fact that we have been through the crisis ourselves which makes us capable of serving others undergoing the same ordeal.

This similarity makes shamanism especially applicable to us on our journey. In a sense, we ourselves are shamans who have experienced the shamanic crises of addiction. Because we have traveled through the hell worlds of suffering and have been delivered to the other side, we are able to act as guides for other members of our "tribe" facing the same challenge.

Michael Harner's book *The Way of the Shaman* is one of the best introductions to this form of the spiritual journey. He also maintains a training program to help bring these ancient teachings to modern Western seekers. Another valuable resource is *The Spirit of Shamanism*, by Roger Walsh.

In this context, we should also mention the work of Angeles Arrien, a shaman of Basque heritage. She is a therapist and consultant who teaches spirituality from a wide perspective, bringing together into one system the ways various world cultures have envisioned the spiritual path. She is also the author of *The Four-Fold Way* and *Signs of Life*, two works on the cross-cultural aspects of spirituality.

NATIVE AMERICAN SPIRITUALITY

As many seekers cast off the trappings of old religious ideas that have been dysfunctional for them, they are beginning to discover a new realm of spirituality in the cultures of the native peoples of the world. In particular, Westerners are turning to the worldview of Native Americans. They are reporting that this philosophy is frequently more compatible with what they are currently learning about spirituality than with much of what they have been taught previously about religion.

Many in recovery are discovering that their addiction has

begun to have larger dimensions than just personal obsession and compulsion. After these have been removed by the Steps and the Higher Power, what often emerges during recovery is a much more pervasive attachment to the modern Western lifestyle itself. This orientation is fostered by what many are coming to see as their enslavement to the industrial-technical worldview. Besides offering us undreamed-of creature comforts and distractions, this lifestyle is contributing, as a by-product, to what may be the environmental and ecological destruction of the planet.

As recovering persons awaken to this deep form of attachment, they are finding that the spiritual practices and outlook of native peoples are more suited to their own evolving philosophy. They are attracted to these kinds of spiritual systems because they place the highest priority on a harmonious and ecological interdependence with Mother Nature.

Another reason for the current interest in Native American culture appears to be the importance to modern Westerners of finally honoring this tradition, which has been violently oppressed for so many generations. In a sense, Westerners seem to feel that this is almost their *own* deeper heritage and that by embracing it they are somehow returning to their own more fundamental roots.

For whatever reason, seekers report that the practices of native cultures, including shamanic ceremonies, drumming, and the sacred rituals of the sweat lodge, vision quest, and others, are important Eleventh Step methods. The concept of spirituality from the Native American perspective offers an exciting new metaphor for those in recovery who are looking for expanded ways to understand the Steps and to define the Higher Power.

There are many books available that bring to life the spiritual worldview of Native Americans. One good beginners' guide is *The Sacred Tree*, which explains simply and clearly most of the principles of this outlook. Also, Jane Middelton-Moz, a well-known pioneer in the codependence movement, is now devoting much of her energy to bridging traditional recovery practices with the culture and lifestyle of native peoples, who have been so ravaged by the horrors of addiction.

BRINGING RECOVERY INTO THE BODY

Bodywork

One of the time-honored tenets of successful recovery from addiction and codependence is the importance of letting go. Most of us are familiar with the surrender process as it relates to emotions, character defects, and mental attitudes. We have all probably done a lot of work in these areas, either through the Steps or in therapy.

But addicts and codependents are notorious for neglecting the recovery of the body. Ever since the beginning of the humanistic era, psychologists have said that our bodies are the repositories of our emotional patterns. One of the main causes of the crossroads crisis is that we have not addressed the recovery of this vital physical dimension.

It is very difficult to feel surrendered when the body is all tied up in knots. Yet somehow this is what we have been trying to do. Many of us have a long history of trauma and other patterns stored in our bodies. We have become habituated to holding ourselves in certain ways, often as a protective response to, or defense against, what we experienced. On top of this, our relentless ingestion of drugs and alcohol has reinforced these patterns and cemented them in place. It is no wonder we can be working diligently on our recovery and yet still feel a strong sense of dis-ease.

Many humanistic practices, such as gestalt therapy, focus on the release of patterns in the body in conjunction with other psychological techniques. In addition to these is a whole spectrum of strategies that deal specifically with the body. These are what we call "bodywork." There are many types of massage, including the basic Swedish approach, the Feldenkrais method, and deep-tissue work, such as rolfing, all of which are effective in releasing energy trapped in the body. For those who prefer a more gentle and subtle method, the cranial-sacral technique is an ideal way to release tensions and re-pattern the way we hold ourselves physically. There are many books available that can introduce seekers to the practice of body work. Nigel Dawes's *Massage Cures* and Lucy Lidell's *The Book of Massage* are two good examples.

Dance and Movement

I used to be so self-conscious that I would not even dance in front of people when I was *drunk*. In my recovery, even though my whole being was crying out for freedom, somehow I still felt like a prisoner of my body.

It seemed as though my Higher Power was beginning to release creative energy in my life that had all been directed previously toward addictive survival. I was able to find channels of expression for it mentally and emotionally. But somehow I never felt as though I was actually *in* my body. I have heard many recovering people say the same thing, especially those who have experienced some form of deep abuse.

Addicts and codependents are just plain tight! It wasn't until I began to let my body move through wild and uninhibited dancing that I really began to feel like an open conduit of the creative impulse.

One of the most exciting teachers of dance and movement today is Gabrielle Roth. Roth, who calls herself an "urban shaman," is not only a teacher, but a recording artist. Her works are a form of "shamanic rock," which are perfect for the free-form expression that so many recovering persons say is necessary to help them let go. In addition to her music and her teaching, she is the author of *Maps to Ecstasy*.

Gabrielle Roth is a modern version of the ecstatic dancers of the world's cultures. From the whirling dervishes of the Sufi tradition, to the trance dance of the Kung bushmen, to the Dionysian rites of ancient Greece, movement and dance have always been an integral part of the perennial wisdom.

The Big Book says to "abandon yourself." This is a tall order, indeed, if we are so restricted by the tensions in our bodies that it is hard to either relax or sit still. Fortunately, there are many ways available now to celebrate our bodies, which for so long have been neglected and avoided because of our traumas, not to mention abused by our addictions.

Tai Chi and the Martial Arts

Most ancient spiritual disciplines recognized the intimate connection between body, mind, and spirit. Among the methods teaching this connection, which have been embraced by modern Western seekers, are Tai Chi and the martial arts. One of the best-known teachers of Tai Chi is Chungliang Al Huang. He is the author of several books, including *Embrace Tiger, Return to Mountain*. He is also the director of the Living Tao Foundation in the Midwest.

In this context we should also mention karate and akido, which have become tools for many recovering persons to experience a harmonious connection between their bodies, minds, and spirits.

THROUGH PRAYER AND MEDITATION

The Eleventh Step tells us to seek "through prayer and meditation to improve our conscious contact." It stands to reason, then, that some of the most powerful Eleventh Step doorways into the spiritual dimensions must be forms of these two disciplines. As we move away from primarily psychological, emotional, and physical systems and venture into what seem to be more spiritual realms, we are apt to discover some resistances in ourselves.

Fortunately, the treasure trove is filled with gems of prayer and meditation that can help transform our old ideas about God and religion. Since most of us grew up in some form of the Christian or Judaic tradition, let's examine first some alternatives that use a Christian metaphor, but do so in a refreshingly different way than we have seen before.

Spiritual Christianity

One of the most beautiful allegories describing what happens when a religion seems to lose its real spiritual power comes from the Benedictine monk Brother David Steindl-Rast. He says that the birth of every great spiritual tradition is like the eruption of a volcano. The fire and molten lava is like the original revelation, the light of the creative, spiritual power that has come forth from the source.

As the lava flows down the side of the mountain, it begins to cool and to gradually harden until it becomes immovable, solid rock. According to Brother David, this is what happens to religions. The fire of the original experience somehow loses its power and along the way hardens into mere dogma and belief. What is left is the *form* of the original revelation. But the *spirit* of it has disappeared. There is a vast difference between an *experience* of spirituality and a *belief* about it.

The good news is that there are some forms of Christianity today that are alive with spiritual power and that help seekers have an experience of their original faith, rather than just a belief in one. Brother David is certainly a living example of this fire. His books *Gratefulness, the Heart of Prayer* and *A Listening Heart* really bring to life the spirit of Christianity. Those in recovery who have heard him speak report that his discussion of the surrender experience greatly enriches their own Twelve Step practice.

One of the most dynamic voices of the new Christian experience is Matthew Fox. Fox is a Catholic priest who was silenced by the Vatican for speaking out against the repressiveness and narrow-mindedness of the Catholic Church. He has said repeatedly that the Church has lost its spiritual power and is controlled by what he calls the outdated patriarchy, or exclusive rule by the Pope and other men.

Matthew Fox has written numerous books, among them *The Coming of the Cosmic Christ* and *Original Blessing*. In *Original Blessing*, he proposes that instead of being cursed with original sin, all human beings are in fact blessed in the beginning with the pure creative spirit. What a radical departure from what we were taught as children!

That we humans are inherently bad, wrong, or flawed is one of the deepest, most insidious old ideas within the collective unconscious. This is certainly an archetypal level of shame that preexists even our early childhood trauma. We can perhaps begin to see some connections between "original sin," the basic Freudian framework of pathology, and even the disease model of addiction. Matthew Fox's concept of original blessing represents the shift from a sickness to a wellness model of religion, just as we ourselves are moving from a disease concept to a wellness model of psychology and also recovery.

At Holy Names College, the institute founded by Fox, seekers have the opportunity to experience a variety of experiential methods. It is refreshing to see such a multidisciplinary approach being employed in a school focusing on Christian spirituality.

A Course in Miracles

Along with the Twelve Steps, many people consider *A Course in Miracles* one of the West's greatest contributions to the world's spiritual traditions. It is written in a Christian style and metaphor, but its teachings are universal and part of the perennial philosophy. The Course was transcribed by a psychologist, who refused to call herself its author. She believed that the material was a direct communication from a spiritual source that did not originate in her.

The Course consists of three volumes. The first, *A Course in Miracles*, is the basic text of the system. The second is a workbook, with a lesson for each day of the year. The third is a teaching manual, which helps to explain the terms and simplify the learning process.

The text of the Course is written in a beautiful and poetic style and is so full of inspiring and thought-provoking passages that it would take a lifetime to grasp them all. Many practitioners say that the best way to use the text is to read just one or two aphorisms at a time and meditate on their meaning. Gradually the truth of the passages reveals itself, and somehow, through the inspiration of the Higher Power, it is translated into practical use in the life of the seeker.

There are also daily exercises, which can be practiced without the need for a Course teacher. Twelve Step practitioners frequently maintain that these lessons greatly enhance their program work. They seem to be a way to bring the energies of the Higher Power to bear on daily life issues.

One of the main teaching techniques of *A Course in Miracles* is the use of affirmations. Affirmations are "I" statements, which, when repeated either silently or out loud over a period of time, help to change attitudes and, ultimately, behavior. Although in principle affirmations can be powerful tools of transformation, they can be somewhat tricky for recovering persons.

Affirmations themselves do not make what is affirmed an actual, practical fact. They are no substitute for doing the Step work necessary to rid ourselves of our character defects. For example, if I am feeling angry and I repeat the affirmation "I am free from anger," the affirmation, in and of itself, will not relieve me of my anger. In fact, it is possible that the affirmation can unwittingly become a way to avoid or deny the *truth* of the reality of it.

I believe that affirmations can work most effectively for us in two ways: First, when we repeat them, they seem to act as a summons from the unconscious. If, to use the same example, our affirmation concerns the letting go of anger, all the ways that we have ever done the *opposite* of the "I" statement will emerge into consciousness to be healed. In this way, they can be an effective adjunct for Fourth Step work.

Second, if we repeat the affirmation "I am free from anger," we will be confronted in our daily lives with all the situations in which we would usually react *with* anger. At that point, we use the Steps and other methods to really become conscious of the feelings and how they affect us. Ultimately, we can let them go and begin to learn more healthy responses to similar situations in the future.

A Course in Miracles can be a somewhat formidable undertaking, because, for one thing, it is such a voluminous text. A wonderful introduction to the Course, however, is *Accept This Gift*, a group of selections from the original with an introduction by transpersonal teachers Frances Vaughan and Roger Walsh. Many in recovery have found the course deepens and enriches their Twelve Step practice and, at the same time, allows them to feel close to their Christian, spiritual roots.

Unity

Recovery seekers often report that Unity has given them a corrective experience of the Christian tradition. What they seem to be searching for is a place free of the dogma and separatism that so many say were the reasons they were turned off originally. In Unity these have been replaced by a loving openheartedness and a profound reverence for the spiritual mystery underlying the Christian teachings and, indeed, all the world's religions.

MEDITATION

Once again, seekers examining this part of the Eleventh Step are apt to be overwhelmed by the sheer vastness of the subject. It is a sound idea to reexamine the good introductions to meditation, which can be found in the Twelve and Twelve and many other daily meditation books and pamphlets that are published by various recovery houses. Then we can reach out to some of the more popular texts, such as Lawrence LeShan's *How to Meditate* and some of the works by Ruth Fishel.

There are probably as many types of meditation as there are different temperaments in human beings. But with a little perseverance and guidance from within, we should be able to narrow the field considerably to a few that seem right for us.

For those in early recovery whose bodies are still reeling from the chemical poisoning and who are about to jump out of their skins, sitting meditation is putting the cart before the horse. What they usually need is to stick to the basics, especially Step work, as well as working with their bodies. Fortunately, there are some great *active* meditations, such as dance and movement, including walking meditation and breathwork, which are perfect for those with chronic shakes or just plain active physical makeups.

For the sake of time, space, and simplicity, we will focus on those methods about which we have heard the most positive reports over the years from recovering people. Again, this list is not meant in any way to be all-inclusive. But we can use it as a home base from which we can gradually widen our exploration as we become more comfortable with the territory.

Mindfulness

Mindfulness, often referred to as *Vipassana,* is a Buddhist technique using the breath. In this method the practitioner assumes a sitting position and becomes aware of the natural breathing process, focusing on the place where the air enters and leaves the organism. During the practice the seeker becomes aware, or "mindful," of sensations, thoughts, and emotions as they arise into consciousness.

Everything that comes up is then let go of, or allowed to disperse. The practitioner does not have to *do* anything about the emerging material other than to let it pass. Sounds simple, doesn't it? The actual *technique* may be easy, but the *process* of staying focused on the breathing and letting go of the arising perceptions and sensations is amazingly difficult.

The reason that mindfulness works so well for those in recovery is that its principal strategy is based on acceptance and surrender, which are two of the cornerstones of Twelve Step practice. As we become aware of our attachments and addictions through sitting, breathing, and watching them emerge, our next task is to accept them and surrender them up. It is easy for us to grasp a discipline that so resembles the principles of our own.

Jack Kornfield is a very special teacher of mindfulness practice. He himself is a Buddhist monk, as well as a psychologist, which gives his teachings a rare balance between Western and Eastern disciplines. He is the coauthor of *Seeking the Heart of Wisdom*, a good introduction to Vipassana and Buddhist teachings.

One of the great things about Buddhist teachers is their humor, and Kornfield is full of hilarious anecdotes about the spiritual path. His teachings remind me of a good speaker's meeting. He says that the purpose of Vipassana is to "sit your ass on a pillow, breathe, and take what comes." Sounds like a pretty accurate description of recovery and life itself!

Stephen Levine is another wonderful teacher of mindfulness. His book *A Gradual Awakening* has been an essential guide for many of us just learning how to meditate. For a simple yet profound overview of the Buddhist perspective, the classic *Zen Mind, Beginner's Mind*, by Shunryu Suzuki, is a must for all seekers. And we should also mention, for a layperson's introduction, *Everyday Zen*, by Charlotte Joko Beck.

Sufism

During this century, and especially in the past few decades, there has been a flood of teachers and mystical traditions into the West from all over the world. One of the most popular of these is Sufism, the mystical branch of Islam. The Sufi tradition has its roots in ancient disciplines springing from many different places, including North Africa, Persia, India, and the Middle East. This eclectic heritage is probably one reason why it has proven to be so attractive to Westerners.

Pir Vilayat Inayat Khan, the head of the Sufi Order of the West, has played a large part in making these valuable teachings accessible to novices on the path. His classic work, *Toward the One*, and his other texts, such as *Introducing Spirituality into Counseling and Therapy* and *The Message in Our Time*, have introduced a wide range of spiritual philosophy and practices to seekers. He and trained members of the Sufi Order have also been conducting workshops around the country for many years teaching the techniques of Sufism.

There is a strong emphasis in Sufi practices on the more devotional aspects of spirituality, including love and surrender. For this reason, many in recovery have been attracted to these methods as helpmates in Twelve Step work. Moreover, a kindness and gentleness pervade the teachings, making them particularly attractive to Westerners in need of this dimension in their lives. In this vein, another good resource for recovery seekers are the works of Reshad Feild, particularly *Steps to Freedom*.

In the past few years, the Sufi organization has become aware of the importance of doing sound biographical and family-of-origin work in conjunction with meditation and other disciplines. Some of its teachers have noted the tendency of many seekers to use spiritual practices as an avoidance of important interpersonal work. They have called this phenomenon the "spiritual bypass." This recognition of the need to do basic codependence work while pursuing spiritual growth has important implications for those of us in recovery who are considering moving beyond the crossroads.

Siddha Yoga

Siddha Yoga was introduced to the West by the late Swami Muktananda, and the tradition is being carried on by his successor, Guru Mai. This system embodies much of the spirit of ancient Indian practices, including meditation, chanting, and devotion to the teacher. Over the years, thousands of seekers have practiced Siddha Yoga and have been able to translate its values into a framework of modern Western life. It has been an important influence in many radical developments in Western scientific, philosophical, and psychological thought.

Frequently, Westerners have difficulty understanding the guru-disciple relationship. On the surface, it looks like the worst form of codependence—completely giving oneself away to another human being. Our mistrust of this process is reinforced by the many horror stories we have heard through the media about how abusive this relationship can be. However, the true spirit of this dynamic can actually be of great benefit to recovery seekers.

The fundamental principle of the guru-disciple, or teacher-student, relationship is surrender. At first glance, this appears to mean surrender to another person. But in fact, the true meaning is surrender to the Higher Power, or to the Higher Self within one, which is also part of the Higher Power. In Siddha Yoga, and in all bona fide Eastern disciplines, there is no ultimate distinction between Higher Power, teacher, and self. Therefore, when one surrenders to the teacher, one actually surrenders to the Higher Power in the form of the teacher.

It *is* sometimes difficult for many of us to reach the level of understanding where we are able to make this distinction for ourselves. But we close the door on many valuable helpmates to our Twelve Step practice if we reject out of hand all disciplines that contain the teacher-disciple component. What is important for us here is the central prominence of the surrender experience.

WOMEN, MEN, AND SPIRITUALITY

Most world cultures throughout history have pictured the universe as having a dual nature. This duality is often described as a relationship between the feminine and the masculine principles. In their myths and legends, societies have designated some parts of nature as feminine, such as the moon, and others as masculine, such as the sun. In the East, this polarity is thought to be all-encompassing; that is, everything is either more or less feminine or masculine. Here the feminine nature is called *yin*, or sometimes *Shakti*, and the masculine nature *yang*, or *Shiva*.

Carl Jung said that a woman has a deep creative masculine principle within her, which he called the *animus*. Likewise a man has within him a feminine principle, the *anima*. Today, quite a few philosophies of psychology are centered around the need for men and women to somehow balance these forces of the feminine and the masculine within themselves. According to these psychologists, we must be "in touch" with both our yin and our yang nature for optimum psychological health.

Spirituality of the Feminine

On the crest of the wave of the Western feminist movement is a whole range of spiritual disciplines that focus on the power of the feminine archetype and whose practitioners are primarily women. These systems are philosophically grounded in some of the world's oldest and most comprehensive spiritual traditions.

We have already mentioned Matthew Fox's criticism of the Catholic patriarchy. Patriarchy is rule by men. Many modern philosophers, both women and men, point to the political, sociological, and ecological crises of our time as being the result of the dominance of the masculine principle. This dominance can be overt, as demonstrated by the political struggles of women of this century. But it can also be more subtle or philosophical in nature. This deep, hidden aspect of patriarchy concerns itself with the fundamental nature of power itself, and how the world's mystical traditions view this dynamic.

Most of us today would consider power a masculine force. But if we study the myths, creation stories, and cosmologies of world cultures, we would discover that many systems believe that real power derives from the feminine principle. What we refer to as "masculine power" is often considered a secondary and lesser form of force that is but a child of a much deeper and profound spiritual—and feminine—power. This masculine characteristic is also what we might call "egoic power."

Many of the oldest spiritual writings of the world state that the Divine Mother or Divine Feminine is the origin of all things, and that the masculine principle is the Divine Son. Others take the view that underneath the relatively superficial layer of the masculine intellect lies the vast, ancient realm of the intuitive feminine. From this perspective, psychological or spiritual awakening can be seen as the setting aside of the defenses of the surface rational and masculine intellect and an opening to the deep archetypal and mythological dimensions that make up the largest, most authentic, and feminine part of who we are.

Once again, we in recovery, both women and men, can benefit from exploring the spirituality of the feminine. We deal fundamentally with the nature of *power* throughout our practice. At first we focus on the lack of power—the inability of our egos to save us. Then we begin to open to the influx of a new form of power. We get in touch with our feeling nature, and, through the power of receptivity, or *surrender*, we allow a deeper force to manage our lives. If we look closely, all of this tracks with what the ancients had to say about the emergence of the Divine Feminine in the life of the individual or the race.

Today, much of feminine spirituality focuses on worship of the goddess. Numerous practices help seekers access the archetypal realms of the feminine within themselves. There are also methods devoted to developing the consciousness of the feminine attributes as they are represented by the various goddess figures of the world's mythologies.

We have already mentioned the work of Marion Woodman and Linda Leonard. In addition to these, Jean Shinoda Bolen explores in depth the nature of the feminine in her book *Goddesses in Everywoman*. *The Spiral Dance*, by Starhawk, demonstrates ways that modern women can reexperience the rituals, celebrations, and magic of the Great Mother Goddess as it has been practiced for millennia.

The embracing of the Divine Feminine represents a unique opportunity for women to discover and explore their own power. This is especially important today for the many who are in recovery from sexual and physical abuse, who truly seem to need a special form of direct empowerment that only support from other women can provide. But let us not overlook the heartfelt search of many men, who are themselves beginning to discover the power of the feminine within themselves as well.

The Men's Movement

Just as women have seen the need to focus on issues unique to them in recovery, over the years men too have discovered the importance of addressing those areas which seem to be of more exclusively masculine concerns. In particular, much of their work has focused on the problem of aggression, which is almost universally seen as a masculine issue. Men also report needing to discover new definitions of masculinity, as well as needing to free themselves from the psychological influences of their mothers and fathers. In addition, they say they are searching for a new form of empowerment, for which thus far there has been no place in our fast-paced, competitive, and power-driven society.

Paul Kivel, the cofounder of The Oakland Men's Project, is at the forefront of the movement to help men recover from the destructiveness of their own and society's violence. His book *Men's Work: How to Stop the Violence That Tears Our Lives Apart* addresses these issues in great depth. For men working a program of recovery, *Catching Fire*, by Merle Fossum, provides a good interface between the Twelve Steps and specific men's issues. *Against the Wall*, by John Hough and Marshall Hardy, focuses on codependence from a man's perspective.

The so-called men's movement was launched a few years ago by an interview in *Esquire* that author Keith Thompson conducted with the famous poet Robert Bly. Since that time, thousands of men have come together in large and small groups to sing, dance, drum, and tell stories that celebrate the power of the true masculine.

This phenomenon was born in part from a need of men to "set some boundaries" for themselves, much in the same way they have seen women develop a deep identity around the archetypal feminine. Many men also report that they have longed for a way to shed the stereotypical male identity, which they believe has been an inheritance, as well as a curse, of our culture. Still others say that because they have tried for years to be the "feeling man," they have lost touch with the "wild man" within. The men's movement gives them a setting in which to explore the fundamental male archetype as it is manifested through the individual man.

Robert Bly's book *Iron John* is virtually the basic text of the men's movement. Another leader in the field is Sam Keen, whose work *Fire in the Belly* has also been pivotal in the theoretical development of the tradition. *King, Warrior, Magician, Lover,* by Robert Moore and Douglas Gillette, provides a classic archetypal perspective on the quest for male identity. In addition to these, John Lee's books *The Flying Boy* and *I Don't Want to Be Alone* combine the philosophy of the men's movement with basic principles of sound codependence work.

We have already mentioned two authors especially known for their work with the feminine who have also written books about the masculine principle. Marion Woodman's *The Ravaged Bridegroom* and Jean Shinoda Bolen's *Gods in Everyman* provide a unique opportunity for men to explore the masculine from the perspective of well-known women philosophers.

For the most comprehensive overview of the men's movement, many seekers recommend *To Be a Man: In Search of the Deep Masculine*, edited by Keith Thompson. Basically, Thompson's contention is that there are many metaphors for this search. For this reason, he has compiled contributions from dozens of sources so that the male seeker can discover for himself which path seems most appropriate.

BREATHWORK

The use of breath as a vital component in self-exploration is as old as spirituality itself. Whether in the form of chanting, singing, dancing, or sophisticated techniques which alter breathing patterns, practices involving breath have been a part of virtually every world mystical system. Today, this time-honored tradition is one of the most valuable gifts in the treasure trove.

We do not have the space to describe what happens physiologically when one undertakes deep-breathing exercises. But even if we did, it still would not account for the following fascinating observation: *With deep and effective breathing, contents of the psyche seem to emerge.* As we have already pointed out, when this material comes into our awareness, or consciousness, it can then be healed.

When breathing exercises are part of a meditation practice, they are often performed in a sitting position. In these cases the seeker is usually under the guidance of a trained teacher. Other forms of breathwork are accomplished in a reclining position, with the eyes closed, and with or without the accompaniment of music. Here, there should always be a guide or facilitator. Whereas other therapies rely on verbal techniques, role-playing, group interaction, or pataka bats to help the seeker get in touch with emotions, breathwork simply lets the breathing do the work.

Breathwork, especially the method developed by Dr. Stanislav and Christina Grof, has proven to be particularly applicable to addictions and codependence recovery, as well as to the mental health field in general. The Grofs have succeeded in formulating a perspective that combines breathwork with an extended cartography of the psyche, which includes, as we have mentioned, the surrender, or death-rebirth dimension. The most accessible introduction to this form of breathwork and the extended cartography of the psyche is Stanislav Grof's book *The Holotropic Mind*.

Because this perspective holds so much promise for the deep self-exploration of recovery seekers, as well as for the evolution of the treatment field itself, we will go into more detail about it in later chapters.

IN MAKING A CHOICE

There have been studies comparing the effectiveness of various psychological modalities. Interestingly enough, the results revealed that no one method was actually more effective than another. However, what *did* matter was the expertise of individual therapists. What seemed to make the difference between "good" therapists and "bad" therapists were some intangible qualities, such as the therapists' ability to be there for clients. Also, clients report that being loved or accepted was among the most important criteria for them. How, then, do we decide with whom to work? If no survey can tell us, it looks as though we will have to do it for ourselves.

There is a wonderful book by Frances Vaughan called *Awakening Intuition*, which can help us a great deal in our decision making. The most essential aspect of any potential therapeutic relationship is that the seeker must *trust* the guide and feel *safe*.

Certainly, given the powerful nature of much of our trauma,

we may have a difficult time trusting *any* therapist, no matter what he or she does. But if we stay in touch with our Higher Power and ask for guidance, we ought to be able to exercise discernment. There is a phenomenon some seekers call the "red flag"—that funny feeling inside that tells us to pay attention.

Besides feeling a sense of trust and safety, what else do we look for in a therapist or teacher? Many seekers say that the most important prerequisite is that he or she be a *guide*—not a director. The healthier we become psychologically and spiritually, the more we come to rely on our own inner healing wisdom. Of course, in the early days of our recovery we could not trust ourselves, because for most of us, the addiction was doing the talking. Or we were so codependent that we could not make a decision for ourselves and were constantly giving ourselves away to other people.

However, things ought to be changing by now. Remember, one of the promises of recovery from the Big Book is that "we will intuitively know how to handle situations which used to baffle us." Our Higher Power exists in us as our inner healer. As radical as this sounds, we are becoming our own best experts.

A basic axiom, then, can be that we would want to choose only those methods and teachers who do not demand our power and who do not try to fix us. It is time for us to stop looking for some other expert to make things right for us. This is also the main problem with the "guru trip." Any guru worth his or her salt will continually place the responsibility for our growth squarely back on us.

ON GUARD

Besides giving away our power and looking for someone outside ourselves to heal us, there are several more dynamics to watch out for as we undertake these Eleventh Step methods. The first is one we have already mentioned, the spiritual bypass. Basically, the spiritual bypass is an avoidance of our personal and interpersonal work while attempting to get spiritually "high." Sometimes working in the archetypal dimensions can seem quite glamorous. We may begin to feel special because we are having "spiritual" experiences.

Let us never forget the power of addictive denial to persist even in the face of spiritual experiences. Psychological and spiritual growth is not linear. We are not making the journey beyond the crossroads because we have finished with our biographical work. Instead, biographical and collective work go hand in hand and should be done simultaneously. There are always deeper levels of family-of-origin work we must undertake.

The second horror scenario is that in the wake of misguided enthusiasm, some practitioners might decide to leave the Twelve Steps behind and move on to more "sophisticated" practices. None of us has any true inkling of just how sophisticated the Twelve Steps really are. Our most essential task is to incorporate our new methods, theory, and insights *into* a Twelve Step framework. I believe that if we are unable to expand and broaden our understanding of the Steps to include perennial philosophy, or the wisdom handed down through the ages, then we are not ready to take the journey beyond the crossroads.

WHAT CAN WE EXPECT?

It would be natural at this point to try to look ahead and see just what we might expect to happen for us if we undertake any of the strategies we have outlined above. Although we will not know until we actually get in the water, we can pass on some general claims that seekers who have undertaken the adventure have made.

One of the most common—and the most exciting—is what might be called the "capstone experience." The capstone experience is the final touch on some pattern that a seeker may have been working on. It is the piece that completes the puzzle, where the seeker can say, "It is finished." For example, seekers who have been working with abuse issues over a period of time frequently report finally going through the original trauma, with all its emotional and physical insults, including, ultimately, an experience of forgiveness and understanding. Frequently the process can come to a completion in the early stages of deep experiential work.

Another possibility—and one not quite so much fun—is that seekers may just go a few steps deeper into the issue they have already been working on for a long time. "I thought I was finished with that one" is a cry often heard in experiential therapy. For example, seekers who have been doing rage work sometimes find, to their chagrin, that there is much more rage inside them than they ever imagined. If we can remember that it sometimes must get worse before it gets better, or that the darkest hour is just before the dawn, then this situation will not be so disappointing.

In the third case, seekers get in touch with something they had no idea was even there to begin with. They may, for example, be tracing the roots of their fear, believing that it is caused by some emotional trauma in their childhood. Then, in deep therapy, they might uncover incidents of near-drowning or other threats to life that turn out to be the cause of their fear.

Although this can sometimes be a frightening surprise, making a pattern conscious that has been buried in the unconscious for so long can initiate a quantum leap in the healing process. Remember, we are blessed with the banquet table of methods and guides who can be there for us when and if we experience this crisis. Probably no other type of emergence from the psyche so underscores the "adventure" aspect of our journey toward wholeness.

No matter which of these scenarios occurs, it is important to remember that they are all appropriate outcomes of doing Eleventh Step methods. Some may seem more glamorous than others. Obviously, almost everybody would prefer to have a capstone experience than to continue trudging along in some old familiar pattern. But we should also remind ourselves that our Higher Power is in charge. Our job is to accept what comes up to the best of our abilities and to surrender to the healing process as fully as we can.

WHEN IT REALLY HURTS

Our experiences of the light and of ecstasy, when they finally come, seem to make all our hard work worthwhile. And they *will* come, sometimes quickly, sometimes slowly. But we would be doing seekers a disservice if we held out the fun times like a carrot, as though they were the only, or even the main, reason we should undertake this journey. Just as frequently, if not more so, and often long before we know the joy, seekers are apt to undergo some very painful experiences.

Many adventurers report that they have been surprised by the depth of this pain. Often these emergences have been accompanied by great fear, as well as the desire to run. Others say that they felt they were going crazy, or that they had lost all footing in their familiar world. No matter how wide-eyed we may be when we venture beyond the crossroads, we are still entering a great mystery.

At this point, we are forced to rely on everything we have been taught in the program about faith and surrender. And still, it may not feel as if it is enough. So we listen again to the words of chapter 2, "Good News," and remind ourselves that we are doing it right. Addiction and recovery are concerned with both death and rebirth. It is impossible to have one without the other.

World cultures have always known this. It seems to be a peculiarly Western trait, and one especially familiar to addicts and codependents, that we should try to leap from mountain peak to mountain peak, avoiding all the valleys in between. But recovering seekers *know* about the valley experience. The Twelve Steps are a true death/rebirth model, just as many of the world's ancient cultures had death/rebirth mysteries.

As we face the possibility that our shadows may be longer than we expected, we may wonder how these cultures that have provided our era with the gifts of the ages worked with the dark as well as the light side. Just how are the Steps like these ancient mystery schools? And what part does surrender play in the death/rebirth process? These are some of the questions we will answer as we journey back into the past to find yet even more ancient roots of the Steps.

CHAPTER SEVEN

Surrender—The Mystery Of Death and Rebirth

Most conversion experiences, whatever their variety, do have a common denominator of ego collapse at depth.

—Bill W.

If we surrender our conscious will and allow it to be made one with the eternal, then and then only shall we attain to a true freedom. . . .

—Sri Aurobindo

Surrender yourself humbly; then you can be trusted to care for all things.

—Lao Tsu

During the pink-cloud stage, recovery feels glamorous. But as we look back, this episode sometimes seems like the eye of the hurricane. And it parallels our current search in an interesting way. Many of us recall how just the discovery that there really is something more was a tremendous morale booster in and of itself. We could also enjoy the anticipation of embarking into the unknown and the lighthearted camaraderie of shared adventure. Somehow we felt that spirituality was a war we could win easily, now that we knew how to get to the battlefield.

But like falling off the cloud, our initial foray into the use of these Eleventh Step methods can also be a rude awakening. It is almost impossible to be prepared for the intensity of what our Higher Power can bring us from the depths of our individual and collective psyches. The experiences can seem so shattering that we are apt to question anew our decision to begin the journey at all.

At this point, it seems perfectly natural for us to wonder, If we have already been through a lot of pain in our lives, what good will it do us to go back and relive it one more time? We all seem to take as a given the therapeutic strategy of getting in touch with painful emotions and experiences in order to release them. We probably never stop to imagine how strange a practice this must seem to someone from an alien culture. Think about it. When we have already suffered once, why would we voluntarily submit to going through the same thing again? On the surface, this definitely appears to be an unusual brand of masochism. What makes this situation all the more perplexing is that it seems to work.

But there is another way to look at this dilemma. Ivor Browne published an essay called "The Unexperienced Experience." His premise is that when we do deep experiential work, we are not *reliving* circumstances, but are actually living them for the first time. According to Browne, original trauma is sometimes so powerful that we go into a kind of psychological shock as a defense mechanism.

As a result, we do not actually experience the event. We are not there for it, and it becomes unfinished business, or an incomplete gestalt, in our psyche. Then, when we get in touch with the trauma in therapy or through Eleventh Step methods, we are in fact truly living it, or experiencing it, for the first time.

When I began to explore my early childhood through my own deep work, I realized that I had always been in a kind of shock. This shock is a response to a pervasive and overshadowing sense of fear that I can never remember being without. Do you recall any of the old cartoons where the villain runs off a cliff and is about to land in a pond of alligators or some predatory fish? Just before he falls into the upturned jaws of the creatures, he starts running like crazy in midair and somehow barely manages to avoid being swallowed.

These cartoons are a fairly accurate portrayal of how I have faced most living situations. I call it being in a state of "run from" in life. As far back as I can remember, I have been in this state. It is almost as though my whole life were one long series of frozen frames of unexperienced events, due to the fact that I was always trying to escape from an experience before I encountered it. I was never really present for any of them. For example, if I met new people, I did not really *meet* them, because I was in the state of "run from" right from the start. I was like that cartoon character, struggling to get away before I had even arrived.

Consequently, deep experiential work for me has been about unfreezing the frames and about finally experiencing these episodes of my life *for the first time*. When, through some Eleventh Step strategy, we can stand in the light of our own consciousness and encounter each experience of our lives, surrender to it, and truly *live* it, once and for all, then we can say that we are in the healing or transformational process. We are not *reliving* it, as such, but actually *living* it for the first time.

To sum up our introduction to this chapter on death/rebirth and surrender, we again find ourselves extending and broadening our context for deep self-exploration. As in previous chapters, we want to emphasize the importance of providing a safe and reasonable setting for undertaking what will be a powerful and not always joy-filled journey into our psyches.

With this in mind, we will first take another look at our own recovery history and the history of the movement itself. We want to discover whether there is already a precedent for suffering as an inherent part of transformation. If there is, then once again our efforts will be sanctioned by the program itself.

Next, we can look for world sanctions by examining how spiritual traditions throughout history have recognized the importance of death and rebirth. Our final task will be to explore the surrender experience to see if what we already know of it will benefit us in our use of the Eleventh Step methods we discussed last chapter.

ADDICTION AS DEATH

At first glance, referring to addiction as a form of death seems all too obvious. We know that addiction, if left untreated, is fatal. In this instance, we are clearly speaking about the death of the body.

But in a very real sense, there are other parts of ourselves that undergo a form of dying during the active disease process. Think back on the stories in the Big Book, or on any of the speaker's meetings you have attended. Or, more intimately, consider your own addiction crisis. What other aspects that we consider integral characteristics of who we are apart from our bodies were also dying?

Certainly the way our relationships with family and friends are systematically destroyed falls under the category of death. The gradual disintegration of our place in the community, including the loss of our ability to work or support ourselves, represents a form of social death that closely parallels the death of the body. And for those of us who may have previously maintained some form of relationship with a Higher Power, the terrible severing of that conscious contact is one of the most shameful deaths of all.

All of these endings fall under the category of the death of relationship. Whether gradual or sudden, whether in totality or in part, they inevitably parallel the dying of our bodies. But there is another form of death, more intimate than any of these, that in a strange way is more meaningful to us than even the death of our bodies. This one is not about relationship with others, or even with the Higher Power, although these are inevitably interwoven with it. We are referring to the death of our sense of self.

We say it is more meaningful than the death of the body because although we will all die physically—finally and irrevocably—our sense of self undergoes many deaths and transformations while we are still alive. In a sense, we must live with ourselves through these deaths, and so *how* we undergo this process powerfully determines the quality of our life experience. The ancients of all cultures knew this, and they developed specific psychological and spiritual practices to facilitate what has often been called the "ego death."

THE EGO DEATH

Followers of traditional Western psychology are apt to be horrified at the idea of the ego death, because there are basically two very different understandings of what the "ego" is. The first definition comes from Sigmund Freud.

Freud believed the human psyche was composed of the *id*, the *ego*, and the *superego*. The *id* is made up primarily of our basic instincts. The *ego* concerns itself mainly with conscious perception and with everyday functioning. It is also a sort of guardian for the forces of the id. The *superego* represents a kind of unconscious ideal for the conscious ego and performs the role of our conscience.

Using this definition of the ego, we can readily see why its destruction might be a cause for alarm among psychologists. Without a conscious ego self, which more or less keeps the lid on Pandora's box, or the id, the resulting explosion of instinctual forces could cause what is termed psychosis.

But there is another definition of ego, with a more universal application. From this second perspective, the ego is a *false self* that we mistakenly identify with as being who we really are. There are many different ways to characterize this form of ego. We could say that it is composed of everything that causes us to feel separation from others, the Higher Power, the universe, or even ourselves. We might say that it is made up of our character defects, subpersonalities, or patterns that we seek to transform through the Steps and psychology.

We can refer to the Big Book for our most personal and appropriate definition of ego: "Selfishness—self-centeredness! That, we think, is the root of our troubles. Driven by a hundred forms of fear, self-delusion, self-seeking, and self-pity . . ." Nearly every spiritual discipline on the planet has as its goal the reduction, eradication, or death of this false self, or ego. They all affirm that without this death, we can never discover our true self or know real happiness in life.

If we examine once again Bill W.'s story, especially the time just prior to his spiritual experience, it is clear that he himself was undergoing just such a death. Listen to his own words: "Now I was to plunge into the dark. . . . The terrifying darkness had become complete . . ." In other places he spoke of hopelessness and utter futility, and about being beaten by alcohol. And throughout this time, there was always the sense of aloneness and loss—loss of job, friends, family, and, ultimately, loss of self-esteem.

This extremely painful process whereby we are systematically stripped of every facet of our identity, every sense of who we are, is what we mean by the ego death. We may more easily recognize this death by a term we know intimately in our own recovery. It is what we call the "First Step experience." The hellish journey toward a recognition of powerlessness and unmanageability is our own first form of the ego death. Without the First Step experience, we cannot recover.

REBIRTH

We know that following Bill W.'s journey through the hell of powerlessness was a shattering spiritual awakening, in which he experienced a profound freedom and sense of connectedness. When a powerful opening succeeds a painful death, many spiritual disciplines refer to it as a *rebirth*. Again, we can use his experience as a blueprint for the archetypal death/rebirth theme as it has been described throughout the ages.

We can begin to see that the two parts of this amazing dynamic—death and rebirth—are incomplete when examined separately. The full process of transformation requires an experience of both of them. This sentiment is echoed over and over again in the AA texts. We have memorized the slogans: "Surrender to win," "Pain is the touchstone of spiritual progress." Indeed, the entire Twelve Step discipline, which culminates in a spiritual awakening, is founded on the death we call powerlessness and unmanageability.

For many of us, rebirth has a religious connotation that is hard to relinquish. We generally think of being "reborn of the spirit" in terms of a specific experience of certain fundamentalist Christian sects. But we certainly have our own Twelve Step language that approximates this concept. The Big Book says, "We have found much of heaven and have been rocketed into a fourth dimension of existence of which we had not even dreamed." Over and over in the texts, we find poetic sayings, which we can begin to intuit are referring to this very powerful and, for the most part, indescribable sequence of death and rebirth.

But we really do not need the words of others to validate for us the reality of death and rebirth. The fact that we actually *live* now at all, in the face of the terrible suffering and destruction due to our active addiction, is more than sufficient testimony. And though many of us came close to actual physical death, many more of us have undergone the sudden or gradual death of our sense of self. What was destroyed in us over time was all that we thought we were—every vestige of pride—all those cherished attributes that we misused in pursuit of our addiction.

The death of the self-sufficiency of our addicted self was followed by our birth into the program's new life. Then, just as Bill W. used the Steps for the rest of his life to bring into actual reality the blueprint of his whole self that he glimpsed in the beginning, we too begin the next phase of our recovery. And this second stage, the part where we undertake Twelve Step practice, is the second important death/rebirth cycle of our adventure.

THE TWELVE STEPS AS CONTINUED DEATH AND REBIRTH

Even though many of us have had profound First Step experiences like Bill W.'s, ones that we can easily call a death, this does not imply that the entire ego death process has been completed. As we said earlier, the first First Step experience, or death/rebirth, is but the forerunner to the much longer, more exacting second cycle. The pink-cloud episode bears this out. What always seems to follow the sense of elation at having come through is the painful realization that the ego has many facets, each of which will go through death/rebirth in its own time.

For some, these deaths are gradual; for others, they are dramatic. What seems to happen in recovery is that over the course of our lifetimes, there is a gradual reduction of our sense of a false, separate self. Within this overarching cycle of gradual ego reduction, there are many other cycles which are not gradual, but which appear to be quantum leaps in our personal evolution. These other cycles are characterized by quite profound deaths, followed by equally dramatic awakenings. Even though the first First Step experience may be one of these, if we continue to practice the Steps, it need not, by any means, be the last, or even the most powerful.

We miss the full power of recovery, and we set ourselves up for confusion and disappointment, if we assume that the major changes are over. *The Twelve Steps are a death/rebirth discipline*. And even though many people in the program experience only the gradual awakening, or the gentle transitions that may not even feel like much of a death at all, still there is within the capacity of the Steps the power of radical death and rebirth. The Steps were never designed for us just to feel good. Yes, we are told we can be "happy, joyous, and free," but the Promises will only come true through the process of continued ego reduction. And when ego reduction reaches that part of the cycle where it becomes dramatic, we call it a death.

We are now discovering that transformation can certainly become dramatic when we utilize Eleventh Step methods. And we are perhaps also realizing that this must be the third cycle of death/rebirth we must face, beyond our arrival at the foot of the Steps and our subsequent early attempts at climbing them. As we partake of any of these practices from the banquet table, the door swings wide on the world's mystical traditions. Within the collective dimensions of the psyche, we come face-to-face with all the ways that world cultures have ever experienced the all-important ego death.

As the methods bring us experiences in the metaphors of different cultures, our journey takes on the qualities of an epic or world search or odyssey. Now that we are gradually awakening to the universality of this experience of death and rebirth, let's take a look at just how some of these cultures experienced it for themselves. Then we will be in a position to explore the key to all the methods—the surrender experience.

MYSTERY SCHOOLS

One of the primary characteristics of ancient spiritual disciplines was a profound understanding and respect for the cyclical nature of life. To a great extent, they adhered to the philosophy that human psychological and spiritual growth followed the same trajectory as these cycles of ebb and flow. Therefore, they often based their systems on well-known cyclical themes, such as the change of seasons, day and night, sun and moon, and, of course, birth and death.

In many parts of the world, societies developed practices whereby seekers could undergo an experience of psychological death and rebirth. These practices were considered sacred rituals and were often held in the greatest secrecy. Novice seekers were initiated by priestesses, or by the *hierophant*, into what came to be known as *the mysteries*. These initiates then carried on the secret and generally oral tradition, keeping it separate from the religion of the public. In light of this, these exclusive societies of practitioners came to be known as "mystery schools."

At this point, we can make a distinction between two types of intoxication. On the one hand, there's the destructive intoxication of alcohol. On the other is the profound release of deep emotions that culminate in being happy, joyous, and free. Obviously, this distinction can tell us a lot about our own story of addiction and recovery. It echoes Carl Jung's assertion that addiction is a thirst for wholeness, not just a disease or aberration. Some form of ritual ecstasy seems to be vital for human psychological and spiritual transformation. *Our own misguided search for this ecstasy through our active addictions can and should be redirected into other nondrug expressions of this joy. And this is one of the primary purposes of our own deep search.*

We receive even more profound validation for our new adventure from some of the most famous of the Greek philosophers, such as Plato and Aristotle. These pioneers of Western civilization were known to be mystery-school initiates themselves. In his dialogue *Phaedros*, Plato spoke of different types of madness, which he associated with certain gods and goddesses. Some madnesses, he said, were derived from physical illness, and others were spiritual in nature. Plato advocated wild dancing and powerful physical expression as an appropriate way to release archetypal energies from the psyche. Such activities prevented those energies from producing that madness which is psychosis.

His disciple, Aristotle, developed the concept of *catharsis*, or the profound release of emotions from the deep unconscious, which results in a state of serenity and peace. The findings of these two philosophers not only provide a context for modern deep self-exploration, but also validate articulately our own desire to continue our search using the Twelve Steps. The fact that Plato and Aristotle are recognized as two of the primary architects of the entire Western philosophical tradition gives even more credence to our exploration of mystery schools as extensions of Twelve Step work.

Among the mystery schools of ancient Greece were the Eleusinian mysteries, based on the myth of the mother goddess, Demeter, her daughter, Persephone, and Pluto, the lord of the underworld. There was also in Greece the cult of Orpheus, which focused on this mythological divine musician's journey into the underworld to rescue his lover, Eurydice, from death. In another ritual the dismemberment, death, and rebirth of the god Dionysus is celebrated as an example of psychological death and rebirth. In Greece, Egypt, Phoenicia, and Byblos were celebrated the rites of the god Adonis; these were also reenactments of the timeless process of decay, change, and new growth.

There were mystery schools in other parts of the world as well. For example, in Egypt, seekers were initiated in the temples of Isis and Osiris. In one of these myths, Osiris is killed and dismembered by his brother Set and later brought back to life by his sisters, Isis and Nephthys. From a psychological perspective, dismemberment refers to the development of our isolated ego selves, composed of patterns or subpersonalities, which become cut off and separate from us. Then, following deep psychological work in which we make conscious all these separate parts of our selves, we experience the "re-memberment," or integration, process. From another perspective, God, or the Higher Power, is dismembered in the diversity of creation, and in recovery, we "re-member" the process into a wholeness again. Along with the

Egyptian culture, Nordic, Aztec, Mayan, Mithraic, and Druidic cultures all had mystery schools based on death and rebirth.

In the twentieth century, Western society's rediscovery and interest in the ancient mystery schools resulted from the consciousness research movement. During deep experiential psychotherapy and self-exploration, researchers and seekers used such methods from the treasure trove as meditation, shamanic drumming, psychedelics, and breathwork, and spontaneously experienced the emergence of many of these mythological themes, as well as reenactments of mystery-school rituals. These experiences came as part of their own profound psychological transformation, in which they often reported undergoing the suffering of a death and the subsequent liberation of a rebirth.

We mention this inner work of consciousness researchers to demonstrate that there is already a precedent set in our time for experiencing the positive benefits of psychological death and rebirth. Moreover, the fact that this is occurring within the context of these ancient mystery schools further sanctions our own efforts as we undertake the Eleventh Step methods.

It is not our purpose in making this journey through the deeper levels of the Steps to *try* to have mystery-school experiences emerge from our psyche. What *is* important is that for millennia, death/rebirth experiences have been important vehicles for becoming happy, joyous, and free. If and when they *do* emerge in our own deep work, we can then welcome them, in all their pain and ultimate joy, as important gifts from our Higher Power.

THE TWELVE STEP MOVEMENT AS A MYSTERY SCHOOL

What is even more fascinating than the possibility of our experiencing a mystery school from some ancient time is that, in a very profound way, we have *already* been a part of one ever since we began recovery. I believe that the Twelve Step movement represents modern society's contribution to the world's great mystery traditions. Let's take a look at how this is so.

We have already mentioned that the mysteries were practiced in secret and were kept separate from the religion of the majority.

These two distinct functions, one for the masses and one for the initiates, were known as the "exoteric" and "esoteric" levels. *Exoteric* means external, outside, or popular, and refers to the part of the school in which practitioners followed the letter of the teachings. Exoteric practice concerned itself with the literal interpretation of doctrine. On the other hand, *esoteric* study dealt with the hidden, veiled teachings that are only symbolically conveyed in the surface, or exoteric, renderings.

Each school consisted of these two levels. Often, seekers began by studying the exoteric philosophy. When they had mastered the everyday rituals, or the dogma, of the society, they became eligible to enter the esoteric mysteries. Then they were initiated into the secret rites, where they underwent the quantum leap in their own psychological and spiritual evolution through a ritual experience of death and rebirth.

If we look beneath the surface, we can see that Twelve Step fellowships function in much the same way as these ancient societies. They too have an exoteric and esoteric level to their practice. But there is one important difference: in most mystery schools, we could say that the exoteric level is *religious* and the esoteric dimension *spiritual*. However, Twelve Step fellowships function as mystery schools, with *two spiritual levels*. Both the exoteric and esoteric parts of Twelve Step programs concern themselves with deep mysteries.

Seekers come into the program not because they are searching for the deep mysteries of life, but because they are miserable, or because they are dying of addiction. However, once they are part of a fellowship, they unwittingly undertake a most profound spiritual practice that carries them far beyond their initial goal of mere abstinence. In this instance, the outside world is like the exoteric level, and coming into the program represents being initiated into the esoteric mysteries.

As we discussed before, the transition from active addiction to entering the fellowship represents a form of death and rebirth. After seekers join a fellowship, they commence to undertake the discipline of the Twelve Steps. This practice begins anew the process of psychological death—what we in the fellowship call painful ego puncturing. Through the Fourth and the Fifth Steps, we face our defects and bare ourselves to another. We begin to learn the value of surrender and other concepts that are an integral part of world spiritual systems, such as prayer, meditation, and service.

All of this deep psychological work is done quietly, without fanfare. Members of the fellowship come from all walks of life and from every stratum of society. It is also interesting that anonymity is a form of secrecy that closely resembles the hidden nature of ancient rites. Practitioners go about their business in the world, hardly ever parading the fact that they are part of a special society. Yet they are known by the fruits of the practice they have undertaken. In every way this kind of spirituality-in-action resembles what we know of how members of past mystery schools functioned in their world.

Yet in Twelve Step practice there is a deeper level that practitioners may aspire to. This is the one characterized by the "crossroads crisis" and the question, Is this all there is? It is the level we ourselves are now approaching as we make the decision to follow the lead of our Higher Power. This is the deep mystery of the Steps themselves—how they might work far beyond our old understandings of reality, on into the collective or transpersonal dimensions of the psyche.

Often in ancient times the mysteries were practiced in what was called the "inner temple." Another metaphor we could use for the crossroads crisis is that we too are approaching the door to the temple. Ram Dass, the contemporary teacher we have mentioned earlier, is fond of relating an old saying from the East: "The lions that guard the gates to the temple become fiercer the closer we get."

Some of these lions are our fears—the fear that we may get drunk, go crazy, or lose everything we have, including our friends. Others are the subtle traps of our egos, which tell us things like "Who do we think we are to be questioning the program and to be dealing with *spiritual* matters?" Or "We were never meant to be *really* happy, joyous, and free." These dilemmas that we face are like the trials that novices confronted in ancient times to ascertain their readiness and willingness to undertake the exacting practices of the mysteries. We can read of the peace or ecstasy they found once they had faced these fears and entered the door to the temple. Once again their stories can be our way-show-ers.

As we stand at the door ourselves, we have the eternal and ever-present choice to turn away or to go forward. We are on the brink of perhaps more struggle than we have known, but we are also on the edge of the most complete fulfillment of the promises we could ever have imagined. We can now see that these two go hand in hand. Therefore, as we have said many times before, let us do as the Big Book suggests and *abandon* ourselves to our Higher Power. In this willingness to deepen our surrender lies the key to the mystery of death and rebirth.

BIOLOGICAL BIRTH AND THE DEATH/REBIRTH PROCESS

In chapter 5, "New Maps," we discussed at length the extended cartography of Dr. Stanislav Grof and how it is turning out to be a perfect structure for practitioners who are moving deeper into the mysteries of the Steps. To reiterate briefly, Grof's map consists in part of a biographical and a transpersonal level, much in the same manner as that which Carl Jung described.

But what distinguishes Grof's cartography from all others is his inclusion of the perinatal, or birth level, which acts as an interface, or dimension doorway, between the biographical and transpersonal bands. According to Grof, within the perinatal level is not only the record of our biological birth, but also all the material that is associated with psychological and spiritual death and rebirth.

Breathwork, as we discussed in chapter 6, "The Treasure Trove," is a modern rendition of the many time-honored spiritual and psychological practices that have used some form of the breath. It is a catalyst that enables seekers to enter a non-ordinary state of consciousness.

To use a metaphor with which we are already familiar, by paying attention to the breath and increasing the rhythm slightly, the veil parts on the deeper dimensions of the psyche. This is done in a reclining position, with the eyes closed. In this manner seekers are able to have a variety of experiences, from an intensification and release of physical sensations or emotions, to insights and visions from either the biographical, perinatal, or transpersonal realms.

After I experienced breathwork, I became interested in the experience of my own biological birth and its relationship to the death/rebirth process. But, more importantly, I have been fascinated by the implications of birth in terms of addiction and recovery and, in particular, what part surrender plays in reliving birth or a metaphorical death/rebirth sequence.

Not only has this practice enhanced my own recovery, but since 1985 I have also had the opportunity of working with thousands of recovery seekers utilizing breathwork. They also report that reliving their biological birth has greatly deepened their understanding of the Steps and surrender. *I have come to believe that undergoing psychological death/rebirth in conjunction with reliving physical birth represents the most practical, applicable, and powerful link between traditional Twelve Step practice and perennial philosophy available for recovery seekers today.*

Many seekers report that they have been able to experience deeper levels of program principles as they relive their birth in deep work. For example, one stage of the biological birth is the time the fetus spends in the womb. It is often relived as being safe and nourishing. This time corresponds to the innocence that exists before struggle. It is also similar to the pink-cloud phase, where we seem to be given a respite before we begin the struggle of further recovery.

In another stage, the fetus is stuck in the birth canal, and there is no way out. There is the sense of being cast out or abandoned. Here seekers experience hopelessness and futility and what many feel is the root of victimhood. *This is the blueprint of powerlessness.*

In the third stage, there is a light at the end of the tunnel. Whereas the suffering of the second stage seems meaningless, there is at least some purpose to the pain of the third stage. Instead of there being no exit, at last there is a way out. A seeker reliving the third stage often gets in touch with issues of aggression and sexuality.

The border between the third and fourth stage is a crucial phase in both physical birth and the death/rebirth process. This is the place of the *ego death*. When seekers undergo this stage of the birth in deep experiential work, all the struggle to get through culminates in agonizing desperation and futility. There is the feeling of being utterly destroyed, and of the complete annihilation of the entire sense of self. They say that this experience reminds them of the last days of their active addiction or some of the hard days in treatment.

This is the surrender point. Often practitioners report that they undergo one of the ritual experiences of death as it is characterized in the mystery schools. Or they go through what actually feels like a reliving of an actual physical death. This death is then closely followed by the fourth stage, or *rebirth*. In the case of the biological delivery, the fourth stage is the actual birth. In the birth or rebirth phase, seekers frequently report feelings of profound relaxation, peace, and bliss.

What we can learn from reliving our birth is that we have all been born *anatomically*, but we have not been born *emotionally*. The shock of the birth trauma is so powerful that we enter life anything but a "clean slate," as Freud said. The record of the birth seems to act as a lens, colored by the nature of our own particular experience, through which we then experience our early postnatal and family-of-origin existence. What we are discovering is that there are other very powerful events deeper than even our earliest moments on the planet that have directly influenced our life trajectory.

We have always known that we must, in a sense, clear our biography in order to be psychologically and spiritually healthy. But we are now coming to understand that we must also make conscious our perinatal, as well as the transpersonal, dimensions. Our family of origin turns out to be not *the one cause* of our dysfunction, but only *relatively causal*. We now know that there are other levels of causality as well.

We have only barely touched on the richness and the importance of the perinatal dimension for our continued deep self-exploration. It would take another volume to explore all the implications of the biological birth process for addiction and recovery. But for our purposes here, we can at the very least stress that reliving biological birth through Eleventh Step methods has proven for thousands of recovery seekers to be one of the most important extensions of their Twelve Step process. This is particularly the case in the deepening of the surrender experience and in ego reduction, which ensues as the result of the death/rebirth process.

THE MYSTERY OF SURRENDER

Of the many universal principles that together create the Twelve Steps, perhaps none is more important than surrender. Surrender underlies the entire philosophy from the First Step onward. And at each Step, it somehow opens the door on the next one. Like recovery itself, the power of surrender seems to be an ever-widening horizon that no one has yet found the limits of.

Dr. Gerald May explores surrender in his book *Addiction and Grace*. While he uses a primarily Christian metaphor, Dr. May still keeps intact the truth of its fundamental *mystery*. Along with the concept of spirituality in general, surrender definitely falls into the category of the "X-factor," or the "uncertainty principle," in the recovery equation.

Many seekers in recovery talk about the time when they surrendered. Around meeting tables, we often hear "Just surrender" given as advice. Now T-shirts with "I surrendered" on them are pretty common. Although we *think* we understand what they mean, some of us still find these references to surrender confusing. They seem to imply that surrender is something that we *do* instead of something that *happens*.

Have you ever sat down and tried to surrender? To actually try to surrender is like trying to pick ourselves up by our own bootstraps. It is literally impossible to do. If we could actually accomplish it, then the whole purpose and meaning of surrender would be something entirely different from what it is. Surrender is an experience that happens to us *after* we have done everything we can either to make it happen or to prevent it from happening.

This is where surrender becomes a mystery. For if we are powerless to create it ourselves, then it must come from the Higher

Power as a *gift*. And because we sense that this gift has nothing to do with any merit on our part, having been freely dispensed by our Higher Power, we say that surrender is a grace.

Still, some may wonder, Well, I may not be able to make surrender happen, but there must be *something* I can do to earn it. It sure is difficult to really let go! If we could do even a *little* something, then it would prove that we at least played *some* active part in the process or exerted a measure of control over the transaction. Although this is an amazingly difficult principle to grasp fully, surrender is beyond the realm of "doing" altogether. It emerges from a place of "non-doing" independent of us, in its own time and in its own way.

One of the most beautiful examples of the surrender experience and the mysterious relationship between humans and the Higher Power is on the ceiling of the Sistine Chapel. There the famous artist Michelangelo depicted a scene with God reaching down to Adam. The most frequently reproduced portion of this painting is the image of the outstretched hands and fingers of Adam reaching upward to God and God reaching downward to him.

In this image lies the heart of the mystery of surrender. After I had seen this picture once and would play it back across my memory, I somehow envisioned Adam as stretching out his hand, and almost his whole being, in a poignant posture of longing and striving. And then I remembered God reaching down to answer the cry of Adam's soul. Well, the next time I looked closely at the painting, I realized that it was quite different from my memory of it.

In actuality, Adam seems *very* relaxed and is half-heartedly holding out his hand, to nobody in particular, while *God* is the one putting all the effort into reaching down to touch Adam. This different, more accurate image, really puts our relationship with the Higher Power in perspective! In the face of the awesome power of grace, what efforts we make toward developing a conscious contact with the Higher Power will always be small in comparison. The mystery of the Higher Power will always vastly outstrip our own desire and ability to reach for that contact.

But in the striking image of the two outstretched hands lies the mystery of surrender. Adam, the archetypal human, reaches to the best of his ability, and desires to make contact. And God, in that Power's own way and time, reaches down. *But the two hands do not touch.* That small space between their outstretched fingers is the mystery point, the arc of grace that sparks across the gap and enfolds Adam in the experience of surrender. The magic happens beyond the farthest point of Adam's reaching. In that empty space, past all doing and knowing, is the grace of surrender.

If we cannot make surrender happen, still there are conditions that render its occurrence more conducive. Among the most powerful of these is the onset of the ego death. Suffering, and the destruction of the old, make way for the rebirth of the new. Surrender is the key to this transformation.

I will never forget my "wasteland experience," the First Step episode that finally brought me into the program. I was not even trying to quit drinking. But somehow, as a culmination to an entire history of circumstances, my Higher Power graced me with surrender. Perhaps at some unconscious level I had had enough. Maybe 51 percent of me finally wanted to get sober and 49 percent did not. But these are just theories. The bottom line is that surrender *happened* to me that day.

Since that time, whenever I have been in a crisis I could call a death, I have brought that surrender to mind and wondered, How did that happen? I guess part of me still would like to be able to find the magic surrender formula so that I can have surrender at my disposal when I need it. But whenever I try to re-create what seemed to work for me just prior to my last surrender, I discover that what I did never works again. I can't fool my Higher Power that easily!

Yet we find ourselves in good company going through these surrender machinations. It turns out that this is pretty much what the recovery pioneers did too. Remember that Bill W. had his surrender experience before the Steps were written. We can almost imagine them wondering, as they formulated the Twelve Steps, How does this work? How can we make it happen again? As a result of their desire, we now have the Twelve Steps, which are specifically designed to facilitate a surrender experience. It was the best formula they could come up with to help re-create a situation whereby surrender might happen again.

We use the word *facilitate* in speaking of a surrender experience because, as we know, we cannot force it to happen. But we can prepare ourselves. We can till the soil of our own being, break up our old hardened patterns, and leave ourselves pliable for the influx of grace. We can exercise willpower in the form of intense willingness, and we can work the Steps as best we can. Or we can use the prayer of St. Francis and seek to become an instrument of the Divine Will. These practices, in and of themselves, will not guarantee us a surrender at any particular time. But we can be certain of what our own responsibility in the surrender mystery is.

We are required to reach as high as we are able, with as much willingness as we can muster. We can imagine ourselves as a vessel, using the Steps to empty us of our own egos so that we can be filled with grace. Or we can open ourselves as a flower, as wide as we can, to make room for the light of surrender to shine through. And once we have done all these things, we can pray for the grace of surrender—and for acceptance if it does not come. Whether surrender happens or not, if we practice our program the way it has been outlined for us, we fulfill the requirements of our part of the mystery. The rest is in the hands of our Higher Power.

SURRENDER AND THE JOURNEY BEYOND THE CROSSROADS

As we know from our practice of the program, the Third Step suggests that we make a decision to surrender. The way we till the soil of our being to prepare for the surrender experience is to work the rest of the Steps persistently. One characteristic of successful program practice is our realization that more and more frequently, we *feel* surrendered. Feeling surrendered goes hand in hand with giving up control, struggling less, and experiencing a greater degree of serenity.

But as we have already mentioned, sometimes the very opposite of this occurs. Instead of surrender allowing us to feel more serene, it might, in fact, initially bring us more pain. Often the control that we exercise and the tightness we feel, both emotionally and physically, are holding down material in our unconscious. As we have learned, this material may well be biographical, but it can also be perinatal or transpersonal. Our willingness to let go and to work the Steps, or to undertake some form of therapy, often acts as a summons from our deep psyche. It parts the veil, opening the way for the emergence of the unconscious material.

In the healing process, the contents of the psyche become mobilized and rise into our awareness. This emergence can be either gradual or dramatic. In either case, as the patterns emerge, we feel them as so-called symptoms. The symptoms are conditions, such as restlessness and dis-ease, intensification of emotions, and often a tightness and constriction in our bodies.

Consequently, for those of us who are using Eleventh Step methods to journey beyond the crossroads, surrender poses quite a dilemma. On the one hand, we can honestly admit that we are probably working our programs pretty well. But instead of enjoying the fruits of this, we find ourselves homesick for a farther horizon. Then when we continue to practice our willingness to open and surrender, instead of being released, we are thrown into a surprising and altogether uncomfortable death process. This is usually more painful than anything we have faced so far in our recovery. It seems as though we are being rewarded for our efforts with an increase of suffering instead of a release from it.

This is one of the finest ironies of Twelve Step practice. If we are not surrendered, we hurt. If we let go, material comes up and we hurt some more. The difference is that once we truly face the ego death, then we can know the real freedom of rebirth. Moreover, once we have practiced these Eleventh Step methods for a while and have made conscious more of the material from our deep psyches, it is easier to feel more surrendered. We must let off the built-up pressure first, and then stay open to the following gradual flow of patterns into our consciousness. The longer we practice this openness, the easier it becomes to stay that way on a daily basis.

We hear over and over again that we must practice the Third Step often. But can we imagine what it must be like to be constantly focused, on a moment-to-moment basis, on the decision to turn our lives over? Our lives would become a constant prayer.

To be that open and surrendered in every moment is surely one of the far goals of deep Twelve Step work. And the only way for us to be this free is to practice the Steps, even if they take us into the mysteries of birth and death. Only then can we truly say that we have abandoned ourselves.

Living more fully in the moment-to-moment process of surrender is, we believe, one of the fruits of journeying beyond the crossroads. It certainly gives new meaning to our pain and a powerful reason to face what mystics have called "the dark night of the soul." We have stood at the door of the temple, and we have hesitated. Finally, we have summoned the accumulated power of our own practice and that of thousands of others, all the way back to the program's founding. We have stepped through the door, and begun the adventure of the mysteries. We have perhaps known a greater struggle, but we have also experienced the freedom of coming through. Now it is time to take a look at the fruits we can expect from our journey into the mystery.

Chapter Eight

The Fruits—Experiences of Wholeness

Dive deep. Otherwise you cannot get the gems at the bottom of the ocean. You cannot pick up the gems if you only float on the surface.

—Ramakrishna

. . . it is certain that all recipients of spiritual experience declare for their reality. The best evidence of that reality are the subsequent fruits. Those who receive these gifts of grace are very much changed people, almost invariably for the better.

—Bill W.

Who will really understand the inner nature of our transforming spiritual experiences, those gifts of God, that opened to us a new world of being and doing and living?

—Bill W.

One of the most powerful sections of the Big Book begins with the Promises:*

If we are painstaking about this phase of our development, we will be amazed before we are half way through. We are going to know a new freedom and a new happiness. We will not regret the past nor wish to shut the door on it. We will comprehend the word serenity and we will know

* The Promises of AA are taken from *Alcoholics Anonymous*, 3rd ed., published by A.A. World Services, Inc., New York, N.Y., 83-84. Reprinted with permission of A.A. World Services, Inc.

> *peace. No matter how far down the scale we have gone, we will see how our experience can benefit others. That feeling of uselessness and self-pity will disappear. We will lose interest in selfish things and gain interest in our fellows. Self-seeking will slip away. Our whole attitude and outlook upon life will change. Fear of people and of economic insecurity will leave us. We will intuitively know how to handle situations which used to baffle us. We will suddenly realize that* God *is doing for us what we could not do for ourselves.*
>
> *Are these extravagant promises? We think not. They are being fulfilled among us—sometimes quickly, sometimes slowly. They will always materialize if we work for them.*

We are no doubt in a very special phase of our recovery now, as well. And, as we have found out through the last two chapters, this new journey definitely requires us to take pains.

In our odyssey through both death and rebirth, we have been overjoyed to learn that the psyche is ultimately benevolent. We *can* look forward to things good. We were also promised something similar to this in an earlier phase of our development, and that promise holds true even now. What's more, those who have already entered the door of the temple report that, once again, as the Big Book promises, "We will be amazed before we are half way through."

One of the first fruits of our efforts is a sense of wonder at the magnitude of the spiritual journey itself. As we are freed even a little from the narrow confines of our old egocentric worldview, we are humbled, as well as exhilarated, by the awesome forces of the psyche and the breadth of the Higher Power's universe.

Someone once asked the great scientist Albert Einstein what he thought was the most important question we should be confronting about the universe. His reply was, "*Is the universe friendly?*" That just about sums it all up! If we are ultimately unable to feel a sense of security and belonging in our life, then no amount of knowledge—scientific or spiritual—will make any difference. All our efforts at self-exploration end up being futile gestures.

But the Promises have begun to come true for us. We know

that something good comes from ego puncturing. And we have begun to trust that rebirth follows death, in the same way that seasons change and day follows night. In spite of the pain, *recovery is friendly.*

There is a wonderful array of gifts we can receive as the result of following our Higher Power through the crossroads and beyond. Some of these fruits lie in the fulfillment of the Promises at a more profound depth than we have yet realized. And there are others that are not connected to the Promises at all.

Before we acquaint ourselves with some of the new, less familiar results, let's first take a look at what may lie hidden within the Promises. It is quite possible that some of these results may seem a little farfetched. But if we think back, it was not too long ago that the Promises themselves seemed like a fairy tale. Yet, since many of them have begun to be realities, perhaps one day these deeper mysteries may also materialize for us.

SOMETHING ELSE NEW ABOUT FREEDOM AND HAPPINESS

We are going to know a new freedom and a new happiness.

Perhaps our first great freedom, and one that sets the stage for all others, is not having to take the first drink—freedom from compulsion. Over time, most of us experience the second pivotal liberation, which is not having to constantly think about not taking the first drink—freedom from obsession. The third freedom that the texts describe has to do with the gradual removal of the chains of our more blatant character defects.

Liberation from the bonds of certain actions, emotions, and thoughts represents the new freedom that this promise offers. But in Step Six in the Twelve and Twelve, the authors up the ante for us on just what it takes to strive "for the perfect objective which is of God." At this point, we can begin to ask ourselves, What takes the place of new freedoms and new happiness when they stop being new?

When the text refers to aiming at spiritual and moral perfection, it opens wide the door for those who wish to answer the call of deep Twelve Step exploration. Each day is a fresh opportunity to renew the power of each Step. And each day affords us the opportunity of experiencing *new* dimensions of recovery, including the Promises. Consequently, we should not be surprised to discover that there are further gifts of freedom that come with facing the crossroads crisis.

One of the most powerful of these involves the evolution of our fundamental worldview as we described it in "New Maps." Before we have a spiritual awakening or experience, most of us believe and act as though we were skin-encapsulated egos. For the most part, we experience ourselves as separate individuals in a world of other separate individuals. If we ever *have* an experience of connectedness or identification with others, humanity, or the universe at large, it is generally an isolated occurrence, after which we resume our normal mode of separateness.

But we know from Bill W.'s experience, and sometimes from our own, as well as from our study of science, psychology, and spirituality, that there is also a condition of connectedness, interrelatedness, and identity, which we can access through deep self-exploration. Both these states—the individual, characterized by separation, and the collective, characterized by identity—are valid conditions necessary for psychological and spiritual health.

Therefore, the new freedom that undergoing this radical Twelve Step adventure offers is freedom from *exclusive* identification with the body, the ego, or the sense of separateness. We will also be able to identify equally with the whole. "New Maps" points out that there is now room for the possibility of overcoming our sense of isolation in a more profound way than we would ever have thought possible with our old restricted concept of the human psyche.

Just as our definitions of freedom have evolved, so has our experience of happiness also taken on new meanings. For most of us, happiness originally meant the fun half of the dual dynamic of sadness/happiness. We pursued happiness in our addiction often as a way to escape pain. Happiness was like a safe harbor, which we were always forced to leave too soon.

But we found that, as many recovery sources have said, it is not something that we seek in and of itself, but a gift that comes to us as a *by-product* of working the Steps to the best of our abilities. A new sense of joy proceeded to emerge for us; it seemed to be available to the exact extent that we did not grasp for it. As such, it appeared to spring from that all-important cornerstone of the program, surrender.

Yet other, previously hidden facets of this promise also begin to reveal themselves in our exploration. Along with the gentle, more passive side of happiness, which is similar to serenity, we find ourselves experiencing a very powerful, active sense of joy that some have called jubilation or celebration. Although for recovering persons this sometimes has a problematic association, many seekers call it being high on life.

Frequently, some of our peers admonish us not to get too high or happy because it might lead us back to our active addiction. For whatever reason, they seem to be overlooking one of the most poignant passages in the Big Book, to which we have already often referred: "We are sure God wants us to be happy, joyous, and free." Well, if the Higher Power wants us to be this way, just how happy and free are we talking about? Who sets the limits on freedom and happiness? Over and over we find ourselves confounded by these mysteries of Twelve Step practice.

Fortunately, we are once again able to refer to world mystical traditions for validation of our right to experience more intense dimensions of happiness. In the last chapter, we saw that Plato and Aristotle advocated the healing potential of ecstatic states of consciousness. But we can go even further back in history than this for validation. In the Vedas and the Upanishads, some of the earliest and most sacred texts of India, there is a Sanskrit term, *ananda*, which means "bliss" or "ecstasy."

The ancients believed that the very fundamental nature or fabric of existence was this ananda, or bliss. What a radical concept! They are saying that there is a condition of absolute happiness that somehow encompasses the entire process of creation, including the cycle of death and rebirth and all the joy and suffering that we commonly refer to as life.

Bliss represents the farthest horizon of the program's promise that we will know a new happiness. The ancients have also said that this state results from opening to one of the "power" aspects of the Higher Power, sometimes called the "life force." There have been many names given to this force throughout the ages, among them *chi*, *ki*, *prana*, *kundalini*, *shakti*, *mana*, and the *holy spirit*. No matter what it is called, mystics say that experiencing this force ultimately results in the state known as ecstasy.

Once again, we tread the realm of the mysteries. There is no adequate language to describe what this new happiness will ultimately be. However, some of the most beautiful prose and poetry in the world is devoted to just such an attempt. But we can begin to get a glimpse of this sense of celebration for ourselves. When it emerges, we feel it, not only with our minds and our emotions, but also with our bodies. Lest we doubt that this type of happiness is possible for us, we can once more return to the source, to the words of Bill W. himself: "I was seized with an ecstasy beyond description. Every joy I had known was pale by comparison."

As Bill W. said, this intense state did fade, but it became an integral part of the blueprint of his recovery from that point on. And there are many other stories in the spiritual literature of the ages where bliss is understood to be not just a fleeting wisp of happiness, but a condition that is the daily birthright of all human beings. We reiterate that our purpose in pursuing this adventure is not to make bliss happen. But we do believe in the Promises. We can, at the very least, not shut the door on it, but instead open to it as one of the gifts that our Higher Power just may want to bestow on us.

ANOTHER WIDE OPEN DOOR

We will not regret the past nor wish to shut the door on it.

It takes a lot of effort to try to hold the door shut on our past. We are learning that once we demonstrate willingness to change, the natural inclination of material from our unconscious—our character defects and patterns—is to emerge into our consciousness. For whatever reason, we fight this emergence and develop all sorts of mechanisms to defend against it. But we compound whatever original pain there may be by holding the door shut.

Once we have let it open, however, the sense of release that follows makes it much easier to be willing to keep it open from then on. But at some point in our recovery, a disconcerting thing sometimes happens. As the result of our persistent effort to practice all the Steps, we realize that our past is not what we have always thought it was. The door that was once shut has opened even wider, revealing for the first time the vast, hidden realms of the psyche. The adventure beyond the crossroads has begun.

One of the many transforming experiences it is possible for us to have in deep self-exploration is a sense of intimate continuity with our ancestors. We feel this not just with the lineage of our own family tree, but often with the culture or race from which we have originated, and even with humanity at large. It is even possible to experience our evolutionary connection with the rest of nature—the mineral, animal, and vegetable kingdoms. And, ultimately, seekers often relate experiences of what could be called their "cosmic heritage," where they recognize their kinship with the Divine.

All of this, and, if we trust the reports of seekers for millennia, much more, is part of our past. Our personal biographical history is but the latest chapter in a long and rich saga of who we are as human beings. When, through Eleventh Step methods, we receive even a brief glimpse of some of our deep heritage, not only do we *not* want to shut the door, but we want to fling it open as wide as we can.

We begin to fathom that our past is not just a series of patterns that make up what we call our egos. It is also a rewarding inheritance of the entire human and divine drama. Not only do we not regret the past, but we ultimately find ourselves celebrating it as one more surprise gift of recovery from our Higher Power. Thus, the possibilities of this promise are expanded by our willingness to answer the call of the Steps beyond our traditional worldview.

BEYOND COMPREHENDING AND KNOWING

We will comprehend the word serenity and we will know peace.

We have already used the valley/peak/valley metaphor in a previous chapter to describe how addicts and codependents traditionally seek to avoid pain. We said that our usual life strategy is to attempt to leap from peak to peak, looking for the "good" halves of the dualities.

But recovery begins to teach us the importance of both sides of the dynamic. However, when we begin to experience the archetypal death/rebirth process in our Eleventh Step work, either through a myth, mystery school, or biological birth sequence, we really come to know the true power of this paradox.

The healing which results from undergoing psychological death and rebirth is not the eradication of death from our lives and the final attainment of the state or rebirth. We are able to transcend our *attachment* to the death/rebirth process instead of being continually subject to its ups and downs. In a sense we learn to watch the cycle flow by from a place of equanimity and not be caught up in our own need to avoid death or attain rebirth.

This does not mean that we will not undergo the death/rebirth cycle in our life after that. But it *does* mean that we will be able to "be with" the process in a way that would have eluded us before. This equanimity is what we call serenity and peace. These two seem to go hand in hand with the more celebrative sense of happiness we have already discussed. They each encompass, and, at the same time, transcend, the duality of which we previously thought they were a part.

When philosophers describe how all human beings are part of oneness, it is not too difficult to grasp this concept intellectually. However, this definitely does not imply that we have had the *experience* of oneness. In fact, the actual experience of oneness is considered quite difficult to arrive at.

In his book *Peace Is Every Step* the famous Buddhist teacher Thich Nhat Hanh discusses the goals of "mindfulness," which we described in chapter 6. He says, "Peace is available every moment, every breath, every step." He seems to be saying that peace is a way of approaching every aspect of life. Spiritual teachers from other disciplines talk about the "silence" and the "stillness" that result from meditation on the presence of the Higher Power. Surely, this state of consciousness is what this promise is referring to in the Big Book. As we follow the leadings of our Higher Power, we will go beyond knowing and comprehending. It is a state of consciousness that seems to be at the heart of experience. Finally, we can begin to grasp that this promise is offering us what a spiritual text of old referred to as "the peace that passeth understanding."

GOING ALL THE WAY DOWN THE SCALE

No matter how far down the scale we have gone, we will see how our experience can benefit others.

What makes us able to carry the message is the fact that we have been there. Being there means that we ourselves have undergone the deep suffering of active addiction.

In the last chapter, we dealt to a large extent with "going down the scale" and then finding our way back up. The only difference was that in the previous context, we called it death and rebirth. We also pointed out that the more powerful the death, the greater the experience of release. Many seekers also report that the more profound the ego death, the more connected they feel with other people. It is self-seeking that blinds us to the presence of others.

If this is true, then we can be of benefit to others not *in spite of* having gone so far down the scale, but precisely *because* we have experienced such a profound death. The death of addiction followed by rebirth into recovery joins us to all addicts everywhere. But the psychological deaths that come later, through the use of Eleventh Step methods, connect us to *all of humanity*.

Most of us worked primarily on our biographical issues in the early stages of our recovery. During this personal phase, we spoke of owning feelings. We said, "This is *my* joy," or "This is *my* grief." However, we have now begun to follow our recovery into the perinatal and transpersonal dimensions of the psyche. There we can discover the archetypes of the mental and emotional states that we previously said were "ours" or "yours."

If in the transpersonal realm we experience archetypal grief, we no longer feel that it personally belongs to us alone, but that it is in fact a characteristic common to all humanity. It is not "my grief" anymore, but is just "Grief," the universal characteristic experienced by all of humanity. When we first experience this archetypal level of our emotions, it is a signal that we are truly beginning to integrate them. We are at last transcending our sense of a separate ego self and experiencing our oneness with other people and humanity.

It is from the place of oneness and identity with others that we can be of the most benefit to them. We have long been aware that carrying the message is part of our *own* recovery and keeps *us* clean and sober, even though, as a sideline, it may also help others. But in a similar way, from the level of identification created by profound death/rebirth, we can serve others best precisely because we have experienced ourselves *as them*. Once we have felt our connectedness, we cannot do anything to others without realizing that it affects us as well. Through service, coupled with identification, there is in the final analysis benefit to all concerned.

Again, we stress that it is the experience of the ego death—going all the way down the scale—that frees us. This freedom ultimately allows us to identify with others and have this promise fulfilled in our lives more profoundly.

FINDING THE ROOTS OF SELF-PITY

That feeling of uselessness and self-pity will disappear.

When we enter the program and undertake the discipline of the Steps, we learn for perhaps the first time what it means to be part of the solution instead of the problem. Addiction is notorious for blinding us to the needs or even the existence of others. But as members of a fellowship, we commence the journey out of ourselves and start to experience a newfound, fledgling sense of "otherness."

But the Big Book also says that these promises sometimes materialize slowly. As we proceed with our practice of the Twelve Steps, in particular through the action of the Fourth, we see how we were frequently plagued by many different aspects of ego, including uselessness and self-pity, long before our active addiction began. To help trace the roots of self-centeredness, many of us take the advice of the texts and enter therapy. The codependence movement and Adult Children Of Alcoholics aid us immeasurably in this regard.

Yet even after uncovering all the trauma of our family of origin, many of us still feel as though we are, at least to some degree, dysfunctional. By now, we can recognize this place as the crossroads crisis. Futhermore, by now we might be guessing that just as there are dimensions of the psyche that underlie our personal biography, there are probably deeper roots of self-pity than we have yet explored.

As recovery seekers begin to look beneath their individual life histories through Eleventh Step methods, they are making some fascinating observations. They frequently find that they have located the root cause of self-pity, as well as many other forms of self-centeredness, in certain stages of the biological birth process.

If we consider the logic of physical birth, feelings of victimization and self-pity make sense. Seekers often say that the birth process is like being cast out of heaven. If we are cast out, then one of two things is true. We either deserve it somehow, in which case we feel guilt, shame, remorse, or self-pity for doing something bad or "being bad." Or else we feel that we did not deserve it and that we are being unjustly punished by either the mother or God. In this case, we feel victimized, and, as a result, we feel self-pity again.

Other adventurers report that they confronted abandonment and aloneness as they relived their birth. Still others relate that, particularly in the later stages of the process, they experienced feelings of intense rage and aggression. These emotions are all among the common reactions to family-of-origin trauma that we discover in our biographical work. But as we begin to make our birth experience conscious, we are able to see that this dimension too can engender these feelings.

The perinatal is not the only new dimension from which seekers say that self-centeredness springs. They also report that there are transpersonal roots of this condition as well. As we mentioned in an earlier chapter, myths frequently emerge in Eleventh Step work that highlight self-pity and other aspects of the ego struggle. We already described an example of powerlessness: the plight of Prometheus being bound to the rock. Other myths from the Greek tradition that people report are those of Sisyphus and Tantalus. Sisyphus was eternally condemned to roll a huge stone up a hill and watch it roll down again. Tantalus was forced to experience over and over agonizing hunger and thirst that he could never assuage, with fruits and drink always just barely out of reach. Incidentally, this last emergence is similar to the report of one alcoholic's episode of delirium tremens, in which he said he experienced, as one of his hallucinations, what he called "the archetype of craving and unfulfillment."

In following the roots of self-centeredness toward a possible source, some seekers have recognized a connection between it and the basic problem of human incarnation itself. They report that leaving the unity of heaven and being incarnated as a separate individual is also an experience of great suffering. Hence, we can see that all human beings may have a kind of "cosmic self-pity," merely by virtue of being human at all. This sense of losing the perfection of the cosmic source has often been referred to as the Fall, and is frequently experienced in deep Eleventh Step work as the source of separation, or the ego.

Thus we are able to see three interconnected dynamics of this condition. First, self-pity, as an integral element of ego, is generated by the events of our lives, from childhood through our active addiction. Second, ego itself is caused not just by postnatal issues, but also by the biological birth process. And third, ego and self-centeredness, including self-pity, turn out to be part of the universal dilemma of *separation from our source*.

Following the experience of separation, seekers also report undergoing a reuniting with the source, which results in a more complete reduction of self-pity. In this way, our new adventure carries this promise to its fulfillment.

GAINING INTEREST IN OUR FELLOWS

We will lose interest in selfish things and gain interest in our fellows.

It is safe to say that virtually all recovery texts talk about reduction of self-centeredness as a primary goal. Hand in hand with ego reduction goes the increase in our sense of otherness.

Our awareness of others expands to include even what is happening around the globe. Our increased willingness to open to the experience of surrender, bolstered by sound psychological work and ultimately catalyzed by carrying the message, is the means by which this expanded sense of otherness is effected. Yet during the evolution of our awareness of the world outside ourselves, something else evolves as well. This is our consciousness of who we ourselves are and what it means to be a human being.

At some point, "gaining interest in our fellows" transforms into understanding that we are *one* with our fellows. This realization, which we have said is one of the results of deep self-exploration, marks the further fulfillment of this particular promise. Being given the gift of experiencing our oneness with all humanity has tremendous implications for us in terms of how we will subsequently relate to other people.

In general, most of us, according to our own value system, make certain judgments about character traits and the people who embody them. We usually open to and attempt to embrace those manifestations we feel are acceptable—honesty, purity, unselfishness, love, and the like. Those that we find repugnant, such as greed, hatred, and anger, we tend to disown or to push away from us. The Twelve and Twelve really helps us see the blindness of this attitude by pointing out that most of these defects exist within all of us, at least to some degree.

But seekers are discovering that deep Twelve Step work carries this point even further. They experience how the *entire human experience* appears to be part of them, not just the acceptable traits, but also the unacceptable ones. And when we say "trait," we mean the *totality* of that characteristic, not just a scaled-down version. By experiencing the archetype, or the blueprint, of the human being, seekers find that *every* human condition exists inside us, either latently or actively. We discover that Hitler is not some monster "out there," but that the qualities we found so unacceptable and heinous in Hitler, or "Hitlerness," are an integral part of the human condition *within us* too.

This does not mean that when we discover evil or absolute aggression inside ourselves we ourselves will become like Hitler and act these forces out. In fact, just the opposite is true. You may recall that in "Good News" (chapter 2) we said that what we are not conscious of controls us. Therefore, being able to make conscious these powerful forces of the psyche and work through them in a safe setting ensures that we will not unwittingly play a part in their unfolding in the world.

When we are able to let go of our resistances to feeling our identity with the *entire* human condition, a wonderful thing happens. Judgment and condemnation disappear. When we have come to understand these forces in ourselves and accept them as part of us, then we can no longer judge others. We will not exclude them from the human family, or from ourselves. Through embracing and identifying with what we previously considered the unacceptable elements of humanity, we now find that forgiveness, love, and compassion emerge.

However, if we find Hitler within us, then it necessarily also follows that we will find Ghandi and Mother Teresa as well. What these great beings represent is also an integral part of the human condition. They are not some heights attainable only to a very special few. They are part of the blueprint of humanity and represent horizons toward which we move during our lifetime of practicing the Steps.

Ultimately, gaining interest in our fellows becomes a wholehearted embracing of all humanity and every human attribute. The crowning gift of this promise, then, is the disappearance of our sense of separation from others and our recognition of our oneness with them. We experience ourselves not just as *a* human being, but also as *the* human, not just as a *part* of humanity, but also as *humanity* itself.

THE NEVER-ENDING FAILURE OF SELF-SEEKING

Self-seeking will slip away.

The Big Book is very clear on the importance of confronting self-centeredness and self-seeking. It even goes so far as to say that it is at the root of our problems. Recovery joins the ranks of the world's spiritual and psychological disciplines in this regard. As we have frequently stated, ego reduction, or the ego death, is at the core of many of these philosophies as well.

We have already made the observation that healing the birth trauma is important in an effective life strategy. The struggle to get through the birth canal is imprinted deep in the human psyche. Even though we are physically born, unless we use a deep experiential method to access that trauma, we are not able to complete the birth experience emotionally.

Imagine for a moment what it must be like to have below the surface of our awareness, yet somehow coloring everything we do in our lives, the memory of "needing to get through." We already know how other patterns have influenced us. We also have learned that when we become willing, material in the unconscious moves toward wholeness, or toward consciousness, to be healed. The way we learn about our patterns is to become aware of how they play themselves out in our daily lives in their effort to be integrated.

If we constantly feel the "urge to get through," then even when we have completed something, we will be denied the satisfaction of our accomplishment. We will continually feel the need to achieve something more, always hoping that this time will do the trick. There are many metaphors for this human dilemma. A common one is that "the grass is always greener." The basic philosophy of the great Indian teacher Gautama Buddha is contained in his Four Noble Truths. The Second Noble Truth is, "Suffering is caused by attachment, craving, addiction, or unfulfilled desire." Mystics carry this sentiment one step further by saying that desire can never be fulfilled, but instead must be surrendered.

Joseph Campbell had his own image of this condition. He said that a life relentlessly driven by the slavery of needing to get through is like struggling to get to the top of a ladder, only to find that it is up against the wrong wall. Ram Dass, whom we have also already mentioned, says that modern Western society operates from the belief that "more is better." As addicts, we can definitely relate! We are just now beginning to see how our own individual problem of addiction might be something that is at the core of every human being on the planet. We may perhaps also be getting a glimpse of addiction as a universal archetype.

It seems that the individual birth struggle is being played out on a global scale in the way that social, political, economic, and ecological crises are threatening human survival on the planet. Many world societies, particularly in the West, are on what Stanislav Grof calls a "linear binge." The trajectory of unlimited linear growth is in direct contradiction to the much more ancient and universal death/rebirth cycle. We can certainly relate this to our own addiction crises. The only thing that could transform the force of our own linear compulsions was the death/rebirth of powerlessness and surrender.

SEEING THE WORLD WITH NEW EYES

Our whole attitude and outlook upon life will change.

We can say that recovery takes us out of the hub of the wheel and puts us on the rim. We surrender the central place in our lives to the Higher Power. We are no longer the sun around which all other planets, or people, revolve. We ourselves become a planet among countless planets revolving around the central sun of the Higher Power. This core shift in our outlook and attitude is probably the most fundamental fulfillment of this promise.

Using the perspective of perennial philosophy, change of outlook comes from giving up our exclusive identification with the body and the ego. Once we experience ourselves as being part of the whole, or even the whole itself, we can never be the same again. The greatest change of attitude comes from discovering that we are not permanently separate or isolated, but are in fact "part of."

Another important change of outlook comes in how we view our own history. Before we came into recovery and began to work on ourselves, we were probably unable to extricate ourselves from our own picture. We *were* the addiction, and that is the only story we could relate to. But one of the results of recovery is that we can begin to see our life as a succession of *stories*. We begin to gain some distance from them, like finally being able to see the forest as well as the trees. Working the Steps gives us a new perspective on these stories and frees us from some of their more restricting aspects.

Here are some statements that characterize some of our dramas: "I am an addict." "I am an adult child." "I am in recovery." "I was never loved." There are as many stories as there are seekers.

When we first get in touch with some of our stories, we usually get excited. At last, we are discovering that we are a self. In the beginning we are apt to hang on to the story tightly, because even if it is a painful one, it is all that we think we are. But as we grow in the program, we begin to develop healthy stories about ourselves. And later still we get in touch with the fact that our life is one long series of evolving stories: some begin to lose their power, others take on new significance. Through the process of surrender we are gradually able to let go of earlier, more limited stories in favor of more healthy ones.

But frequently we are unable to let go of a story. At some point we realize that we are saying the same thing over and over in meetings. We begin to feel stuck and maybe just a little tired of our "line." Without being aware of it, we are hanging on to what may be an outdated definition of who we are, when something else may be trying to emerge to take its place. This combination of circumstances is a sign that we are ready to move through the death of one story and into the rebirth of another. I believe that each story remains with us as long as it is important and until we have integrated every aspect of it.

In fact, some stories we do not ever want to get rid of entirely. For example, it is extremely important that we always remember we are addicts. However, as we grow, this story should find its place within the entire saga of stories that make up who we are. We are able to see that we are not *just* addicts, but are in fact human beings first and foremost. We can redefine ourselves as human beings who have addicted selves. We are not just adult children, but human beings who each have an adult-child self.

This ability to let go of some stories and to see others in a new light is a sign that this promise is being fulfilled in our lives. But once we begin to explore the deeper mysteries of recovery, we also uncover other, sometimes glamorous, stories: "I was a breach birth." "I was a shaman in one of my past lives." "I am the archetype of Love." In addition, we can have all sorts of amazing revelations about the nature of the universe: "I now know that there are seven planes of existence." "I know that there are four planes of existence." "I understand the birth of creation." These stories can be so fascinating that we are easily led into believing that we are privy to some exclusive and final truth. We become attached to them and see them as being somehow bigger and better than our other stories of ourselves.

It is definitely true that some stories are more functional than others, and that replacing old ones with new ones represents a moving toward wholeness on our part. But in the final analysis, *they are all just stories*. They are *experiences* we can have from our unconscious that should tell us something about our recovery. In order for us to be truly free, we must, as we read in *Twenty-Four Hours a Day*, be able to "wear the world like a loose garment." We must be able not only to participate in a story but also to stand back from it and let go of it if our Higher Power brings us a different one.

Before we close this section, one other interesting thing about stories should be mentioned. Have you ever heard someone in a meeting, or even yourself, say, "My name is ____________ and I am an alcoholic, a drug addict, an overeater, a codependent, an adult child, a sex addict"? Now, this is a pretty serious story! It sure does seem to get complicated sometimes.

At some point in our Twelve Step work, we will, we hope, be able to see how all addictions are part of one all-encompassing archetype of Addiction. And *everybody* is one. Many recovery seekers relate that when they were able to lighten up a little bit and begin to let go of defining themselves exclusively by their addictions, the power of addiction began to loosen its hold on them. Recovery should help us begin to simplify things.

Ultimately, the transpersonal perspective provides us with the eagle's-eye view, where we are able to step outside our limiting worldview and see the big picture. We come to understand that all stories and all metaphors have their place. This evolution of our outlook is very much like giving up the sanctity of our cherished opinions. And we definitely know what opinions are like! To be able to participate playfully in a variety of metaphors and honor the gifts of *all* our stories, without being limited by any of them, is one of the hallmarks of deep recovery. It is also a sign that this promise is really coming true in our lives.

MAKING ROOM FOR FEAR

Fear of people and of economic insecurity will leave us.

It is interesting that of all the fears we know as human beings, the Big Book makes a promise about people and economic insecurity. For whatever reason, these two seem to dominate us like no others. Although most of us would rather this promise read, "*Economic insecurity* will leave us," we must be content with the possibility of at least being free of the fear.

However, we are also aware that the Big Book speaks of our being "driven by a hundred forms of fear." Now that we are exploring our deeper past, we may begin to wonder if fear too has some common origin from the depths of our psyche. If so, then getting in touch with that level might be beneficial in freeing us from its bonds.

From many different sources of perennial philosophy, we find that fear of death is the fundamental fear underlying all others. In addition, seekers going through deep self-exploration report the same thing. They say that as they trace the roots of their various fears, these frequently culminate in either an experience of psychological death or one of reliving a physical death from what seems to be a past life. Both of these types of death, when undergone in deep Eleventh Step work, result in what seekers say is a more complete freedom from all forms of fear.

The research that is currently being done in the field of near-death experiences is providing amazing support for this kind of self-exploration. In his book *Heading Toward Omega*, Kenneth Ring presents numerous cases of near-death experiences, or NDEs. His findings reveal that in a majority of cases, subjects who have undergone clinical death and who have been brought back to life experience a profound shift in their attitude toward life.

Moreover, this shift closely resembles the peak experience and the ego death. In short, these people often have dramatic spiritual awakenings. The results of undergoing physical death and psychological death seem to be the same—a radical reorientation toward some form of spirituality and *freedom from the fear of death*.

This research really hits home with us in recovery, because many of us actually came so close to dying in our addiction. This is one of the main reasons why the gift of surrender is so profound for us. It is often literally, not just metaphorically, a rescue from death itself. *Obviously, though, we would not want to put ourselves in some form of physical danger again so that we might lose our fear of death.* But we *can* take on Eleventh Step methods that will provide us access to the experiences of the ego death.

This is exactly what shamans and mystery-school practitioners have done for millennia. Just as we have found that the Steps are deep enough to lead us into the realm of birth, we once again discover that they can also guide us into the mystery of death.

LIVING INTUITIVELY

We will intuitively know how to handle situations which used to baffle us.

Around meeting tables, recovery seekers often talk about the joys of finally being "in the flow." This feeling comes from giving up the fight, and from being willing to make our will one with that of the Higher Power.

Some have used the metaphor of surfing to describe our newfound ability to handle life in an intuitive way. When we were engaged in active addiction, we were like a surfer who is unable to catch a wave. We were adrift, while the waves of life's opportunities just passed us by. Or else we were like the famous Persian king who stood on the beach and commanded that the ocean do his bidding. Talk about control!

When we enter recovery, we are finally able to catch a wave. But we soon discover that the waves of change are in the hands of the Higher Power. We cannot control their direction anymore than that king could stop the tide from coming in. If we are not to "wipe out," then we must learn to go with the flow of the wave and intuitively follow its trajectory. When we surrender our own limited sense of knowing, we ultimately discover that the planning of the universe, or our Higher Power, has had a better idea all along.

In a sense we are then able to participate in the unfolding of life's direction, to the exact extent that we surrender our obsession with being the Director. We give up the need to control not only people, places, and things, but also the very outcome of our personal destiny itself. The result of this surrender is a new freedom, as well an awareness of the big picture and a wonder at the beauty of the Divine plan.

HIGHER POWER AS THE DOER

We will suddenly realize that God is doing
for us what we could not do for ourselves.

When we were first introduced to the concepts of "powerlessness" and "unmanageability," we assumed that these terms referred exclusively to our addiction. Our first realization of power as part of the Higher Power came when our obsession and compulsion were lifted. But we soon learned that there was very little else in our lives over which we were *not* powerless, and very few things we could manage successfully.

Thankfully, we *did* discover that we were in charge of at least two things: First, we had to exercise as much willingness as we could to conform to the Higher Power's will. And second, we had to *act*. It is a good thing we are not required to do much else, because just these two alone are the labors of a lifetime.

As we explore the further realms of the psyche, we sometimes bring to light some other, more perplexing things about the nature of "will" and "power." For example, we may get in touch with the archetypes of Will and Power themselves. At that point, we might experience their unlimited nature as attributes of the Divine. But these realizations may present us with some confusion when we consider the implications of the First Step. In the face of such unlimited power and will, how and why are we powerless? Where has all this willpower gone? If we are part of the Higher Power, then why are we powerless?

Admittedly, it is not necessary for us to know the answers to these questions in order to accept powerlessness. However, at some point these questions may arise, not from a place of denial, but from a genuine interest in the unfolding of our Higher Power's universe. After all, wanting to know, and knowledge itself, are both gifts from the Higher Power too.

When we say that we are powerless, we are also eventually inclined to ask the question, What is this "we" that is powerless? Is it the "we" that is connected to the Higher Power, or some other aspect of self? Our experience reveals to us that it is our ego, or the false self that we mistakenly thought we were, which has no power. To the extent that we have operated in our lives with what we thought was the power of free will, we have lost that power in the pursuit of our active addiction. It seems to have been consumed by the energies of obsession and compulsion.

To use the biblical reference of the prodigal son/daughter, we might say that we have squandered our inheritance. Moreover, any sense of a real self connected to the Higher Power was also consumed by the false, addicted self. Any power the false self utilizes has been drawn from the source of all power, the Higher Power itself.

However, once we experience the death of this false self, then there begins to emerge for us our true self. This true self will continue to grow throughout our lifetime practice of the Steps. It is the "I" that emerges more fully each time a death frees us from the multileveled chains of our patterns and character defects. It is a gift of grace. From that point on, we realize we have the power to choose recovery on a daily basis.

We can also experience that all will comes from the Higher Power. From the transpersonal perspective, we learn that there is not only "your will" or "my will" or even "personal will" or "Divine Will," but also just *Will*. Therefore, what we thought was our personal will, which we used for the pursuit of our addictions, is not in fact ours at all, but has been the Higher Power's all along. Our false self had simply "misappropriated" it for its own selfish use.

If the one Divine Will allows itself to be consumed by ego in the pursuit of addiction, then this leads us to look for some ultimate positive purpose in addiction. Many of us have said we are grateful alcoholics. We mean that, in our case, addiction is probably the only condition forceful enough to provide the ego death necessary to turn our lives around. Ultimately, we can begin to envision that ego and self-centered will are all "Higher-Powered" and that their purpose has been to move us back toward wholeness and our Higher Power.

Eventually, we are able to experience, as Bill W. said, our "oneness" with the Higher Power. And when we do this, we at last understand the true meaning of this promise. The reason God is doing for us what we could not do for ourselves is that the Higher Power is ultimately all that exists. The Sufis say that God is "love, lover, and beloved." Other disciplines refer to the Divine as the "doer, the act of doing, and what is being done." This triple dynamic includes the *whole* picture. We are being required through the practice of the Steps to give up the independent sense of being the doer. In the most absolute sense, it is the Higher Power that is the doer. This is what we truly mean by the Higher Power doing for us what we cannot do for ourselves.

The final result of surrender, of "abandoning" ourselves to this Higher Power, will be that the old "we" will no longer exist. And the new "I" will be none other than the Higher Power. We will then be able to live in two perspectives—having a fully developed sense of individuality while at the same time being one with the Whole that is the Higher Power. This truth is at the heart of virtually all the world's spiritual systems. Seekers of all ages, including those who are now exploring these deep realms, report that this experience is possible and that it leads to a more fulfilling life. It is also the culminating dimension of this final promise.

This concludes our discussion of the far horizons of the Promises. However, we said in the introduction that there were other fruits of deep Twelve Step practice as well. Let's take a look at some of these.

SIMPLICITY

We have heard many times that Twelve Step practice is a "simple program for complicated people." It should come as no surprise, then, that one of the gifts we receive for our endeavors is an appreciation for simplicity in our lives. As we begin to relinquish the epic struggles of the ego, our vain hopes and unrealistic expectations, a new world opens up to us. Instead of always struggling to get through, we have more of an attitude of "no place I need to go—nothing I have to do."

Just as certain ego struggles have roots in the biological birth process, so are there positive states that have a causative level there as well. For example, the gentle experience of simplicity that grows out of a profound trust in the safety and goodness of the universe is a basic characteristic of the first birth stage, the womb experience we described earlier. And the peace that comes from surrendering and giving up the need to struggle corresponds directly to the freedom of the fourth stage.

If we use the birth model as a metaphor for transformation, then we can say that moving through trauma into the release of joy corresponds to working through the problematic aspects of the birth and reorienting ourselves to its positive aspects. By healing our perinatal issues, we can make these positive aspects of the birth the new context of our lives. And one of the results of this new direction is our ability to enjoy simplicity.

We no longer have to be stimulated all the time along the way, but find ourselves appreciating life itself. We do not always have to be doing something grand. We can feel comfortable in stillness and quietness, and in "non-doing." Simple acts that would have bored us to tears before, such as taking a walk, being in nature, or just hanging out with friends or family, become rewarding and fulfilling pastimes. More and more we experience life as a process of "being" instead of just "doing."

Many of us admit that the "one day at a time" concept and the essence of the Serenity Prayer have been difficult to grasp. But nothing succeeds like repeated surrenders and death/rebirths to help us learn what Ram Dass has called "being here now." Somehow, we have been able to give up our attachment to yesterday and tomorrow. Ultimately, these slogans lead us into a very profound yet simple relationship with the present moment.

Finally, we should mention another axiom, "Keep it simple." For those of us who consider ourselves complex people, to be able, finally, to experience what this means is a real delight. But we have also felt that this truth poses something of a paradox for us. We have sometimes wondered why we would undertake a journey such as the one we are now on when it often seems to be anything but simple.

We have come to believe that by the very fact that we have kept it simple, and have been willing to surrender as best we can, our Higher Power has given us the gift of experiencing just a little of the incredibly *complex* and beautiful nature of the universe. *Both* of these dynamics, simplicity and complexity, are attributes of the Higher Power. When we look at the beauty of a rose window in a cathedral, we appreciate the power of its intricacy. But at the same time, our experience of the beauty is profoundly clear and simple. We would not turn away from enjoying the window because the art work is too complex. In a like manner, we embrace the opportunity to explore the myriad manifestations of our Higher Power's universe. And the result of this exploration is a return full circle to the beauty of simplicity.

BEAUTY

Another blessing we receive from this new adventure is the emergence of a fresh appreciation for beauty. Just as we are able to enjoy simplicity in and of itself, we discover that we see everything with new eyes, including what we would never have thought of as being beautiful before. Beauty turns out to be like our newfound sense of serenity, peace, and happiness. It is not just part of a duality, but somehow transcends both beauty and ugliness, becoming something much richer than either of them.

There is a Sufi prayer that describes the nature of the Divine as the "perfection of love, harmony, and beauty." If we imagine that our Higher Power is this perfection, then it stands to reason that as we develop a more intimate conscious contact with this Power, we will become more aware of the aesthetic dimensions of life. This awareness includes an appreciation not just of artistic endeavors themselves, such as painting, music, and poetry, but also of the creativity inherent in nature and the fascinating diversity of the human spirit.

Ultimately, it becomes difficult to see such gifts as serenity, happiness, simplicity, and beauty as being separate entities only. In Eleventh Step practice, we can enter a dimension where our separateness from other individuals becomes less distinct and our identity with them becomes the primary characteristic. In the same way, we begin to discern that all these fruits of our exploration are somehow part of a collective gift that almost defies description.

One twentieth-century Indian philosopher, Sri Aurobindo, called this all-encompassing sense *rasa*. He said that we are heir to the archetype of Beauty, in much the same way that we can experience our five senses as part of one archetypal Sense. As human beings with an individual and a collective nature, we have the opportunity in our lives to experience both the myriad flowering of these separate blessings and that state of consciousness which contains the mystery of their oneness. In this way the experience of beauty becomes an evolving adventure that parallels our search for wholeness.

CARING FOR THE MOTHER—INTEREST IN ECOLOGY

The way we as a species have historically related to nature and the environment makes an interesting story. In the Bible, we read how humans were not only created separate from the earth and the rest of creation, but were also given "dominion" over it. This perspective was further refined by Western philosophers of the past two centuries, such as Francis Bacon. Bacon spoke of nature as though it were a woman who needed to be subdued, exploited, and dominated for our own use. We do not have to look far to see the tragic outcomes of this attitude.

Believing and acting as though nature were a slave to humanity is a far cry from the perspective of many native cultures from around the world. These societies see an essential unity between self, the Divine, and nature and therefore treat nature with the utmost respect. In many myths, nature is described as the body of the world, or the universal Mother.

The relationship between the earth and humans is frequently that of mother and children, in which nature gives sustenance to its offspring and ultimately reclaims them in the eternal cycle of death and rebirth. That we speak of the earth's environment as "Mother Nature" is no naive holdover from a child's fairy tale but rather a metaphorical reflection of a truth known to seekers in cultures universally.

Our own deep work in the collective dimensions of the psyche reveals information about our relationship to the planet that is strikingly similar to the attitudes of aboriginal societies. Like those peoples, we also are able to experience our oneness with the earth and with the process of nature. Once we have felt this intimate connection, it is almost impossible to feel comfortable with our previous practices of environmental exploitation. As our attitudes toward consumption change, we are also more inclined to change our behavior and lifestyles in order to reflect more accurately our own internal transformation.

Many seekers are also exploring ways to become involved in the various ecological and environmental movements. The desire to be of service in this important area seems to be a natural extension of what we have learned from Twelve Step work. It appears that many recovery seekers are beginning to carry an ecological message as part of their own spiritual growth.

In the final chapter, we will examine how addiction, as it is played out on a global scale, is one of the principal causes of the current ecological crisis and how recovery represents an archetypal solution to this dilemma. But for now, it is sufficient to emphasize that concern for the environment is one of the natural results of a spiritual awakening.

FREEDOM FOR OUR BODIES

Virtually all the gifts we have described so far have been emotional, psychological, and spiritual. However, we made it clear in a previous chapter how the physical dimension is intimately connected with these other levels of our being and must be included in any thorough discussion of wholeness. Therefore, lest we commit the same oversight that so many of us have often done, we will now take a look at what deep self-exploration means in terms of our bodies.

Many recovery seekers have reported that even though they are abstinent and have found a certain degree of emotional and spiritual sobriety, they still feel a tension in their bodies. They are discovering that surrender and letting go are not just concerns of the psyche. These experiences also refer to one of the most basic and tenacious forms of holding on—the way we inhabit our own bodies. This physical discomfort may be localized, or it may affect the whole body in the form of a general sense of tightness and holding on.

Although there frequently are medical reasons, such as accidents, for chronic pain, other pains appear to have a psychological basis. Seekers are often amazed to discover that after doing a particularly good piece of psychological work, they notice a definite release of physical tension. This release is sometimes temporary, but many report that they have found permanent relief from some pains as the result of doing deep exploration. Even in the case of trauma due to accidents, there is often relief once the physical and psychological elements of the accident that emerge during self-exploration have been integrated.

Once again, we might find it useful to trace the causes of trauma, in this case physical pain, through the biographical dimension, into the perinatal, and on into the transpersonal realms. It should be almost obvious by now that biological birth might also be a causative level of many kinds of chronic pain. Undoubtedly, the acute trauma of birth has to be one of the most dramatic physical, not to mention emotional, experiences that we will undergo in our whole lives. And it happens before we even get here!

In any event, seekers who have experienced in deep self-exploration what felt like biological birth report that many of the pains they have felt most of their lives might actually have originated there. They frequently mention release from such chronic situations as head, back, neck, and shoulder pains, as well as tension in the pelvic area. We are not saying that biological birth is *the* cause of chronic pain. However, thousands of seekers have said that they have experienced significant relief from this trauma by their *experience* of the birth in deep psychotherapy.

Although some of these findings may seem farfetched, their implications for seekers cannot be ignored. For those who have suffered the often agonizing torment of pain for much of their lives, to be able to experience relief from it is to them nothing short of miraculous. We are quick to recognize in the Higher Power the power to change us emotionally, psychologically, and spiritually. Yet we are somehow more reluctant to believe that this power can transform our bodies as well. But many are now learning through this new adventure that we no longer need to limit the Higher Power, that we can in fact envision a much more expanded dimension of that Power's ability to heal us.

WHAT NEXT?

Many teachers have told us, in many different ways, that the spiritual life is not a goal, but a *way of living*. It is not about attaining some far-off objective, such as enlightenment. It is about living one day at a time to the best of our abilities. It is helpful for us to remind ourselves at this point that just as happiness is a by-product of practicing the Steps, these fruits of deep self-exploration are also gifts that we receive independent of any merit on our part. Nor can they be wrested from the grasp of the Higher Power any more than we can create our own surrender.

We are also inclined to become involved in what one modern Buddhist teacher has called "spiritual materialism." One aspect of this materialism is treating the spiritual path as though it were a contest, in which the object is to get more accolades—in this case more promises—than our peers. It is amazing how tenacious our egos are!

But some questions naturally arise: What happens to us if we do experience some of these fruits? What will we be like in the world after that? Will we have to go live on a mountaintop somewhere? Fortunately, there are many who have traveled the Broad Highway before us who can share what they have learned. One of them tells us, "After enlightenment, the laundry." And we thought we would get to be special, and somebody else would have to do the laundry! As these teachers remind us to keep it simple, how quickly we see that our journey returns us to the recovery world we have always known so well.

What we do *after* all this spiritual exploration is pretty much the same thing we did *before* we undertook the journey. What is different is *how* we do it. And how it is different is the result of the way that the Promises and other fruits have become an integral part of our lives. We still take care of business. We work, have relationships, play, and stay *clean and sober*.

Another Zen source tells us to "chop wood, carry water." This seems to keep it pretty simple. And Ram Dass says that if we are lucky, we end up being "nobody special." We do what we do. In a sense our whole attitude and outlook upon life has changed. But in another way, everything remains the same. Once again, we encounter a paradox that is just one more mystery of the Steps.

In the novel by Hermann Hesse entitled *Siddhartha*, the hero spends his life going through all manner of triumphs and trials, including his own addictions, deaths, and rebirths. In the end, after his greatest surrender, he becomes the simple boatman for a ferry that carries pilgrims across the river. This story is a perfect archetype for us on our own journey. The Twelfth and final Step of our practice admonishes us to carry the message. It does that before we take this adventure, and it does so again once we have gone through the crossroads and on down the Broad Highway. Now we too can help those pilgrims who want to cross the river, just as we ourselves continue to be guided by all who have gone before us.

Over the course of this book, we have put together, stone by stone, the structure of deep Twelve Step practice. Our foundation rests solidly on the experience of recovery pioneers. It is strengthened by the gifts of the ages—world psychological and spiritual practice. We have included as much of the big picture as we could, making sure that we have made room for death as well as birth. And we have adorned our structure with the fruits of undertaking our adventure.

In the next chapter, our task is to see how recovery is our culture's most profound contribution to perennial philosophy. It is time to set the capstone in place. This final piece will put the Twelve Steps in the ranks of the world's great yogas, or spiritual practices.

CHAPTER NINE

Stepdance—The Twelve Steps As a Western Yoga

May all creation dance for joy within me.

—Chinook Psalter

Better indeed is knowledge than mechanical practice. Better than knowledge is meditation. But better still is surrender of attachment to results, because there follows immediate peace.

—The Bhagavad Gita

As a society we must never become so vain as to suppose that we are authors and inventors of a new religion. We will humbly reflect that every one of A.A.'s principles has been borrowed from ancient sources.

—Bill W.

Most of the world's spiritual systems have been in existence for hundreds, if not thousands, of years. They have profoundly influenced the course of history and the evolution of virtually all human institutions. Their contribution is evidence of the profound spiritual power that has fueled them since their birth.

Compared to these perennial giants of philosophic thought, the Twelve Step movement is still in its infancy. In the shadow of systems thousands of years old, it has existed for little more than half a century. World literature is filled with stories of famous women and men who have ventured to the farthest dimensions of spiritual realization through the practice of these disciplines. But the program makes no such extravagant claims toward any grand goal other than the possibility of sobriety. If an addict dies clean and sober, then most of us say that the Steps have fulfilled themselves. Yet we are beginning to wonder if the Steps might also be offering us much more than just dying sober. Judging from the last chapter's exploration of the Promises, some additional claims may not be unfounded.

Although the movement is young compared to its world counterparts, many seekers feel that the Twelve Steps belong in the ranks of the great traditions even now. In order to explore this possibility, it might prove enlightening to direct our attention to a practice that has been the spiritual focus of millions for thousands of years and is recognized as one of the pillars of world philosophical thought. This discipline is known as *yoga*. If we can find parallels between yoga and the Twelve Steps, we can then make a strong claim that the Twelve Step movement is a world practice in its own right.

Before we go deeper, however, we need to address those misgivings we may have in exploring such an exotic concept. *Yoga* is definitely one of those words that conjures up all sorts of strange images. Until they investigated it, many seekers thought that yoga was just some strange method of body contortions. It was difficult to see what relevance, if any, yoga had for us in the West, and in particular for those of us on a spiritual path.

What we thought was the whole field of yoga, namely a set of techniques for disciplining the physical body, turned out to be just one branch, called *hatha yoga*. But yoga is infinitely more vast and complex than this. The majority of yoga schools focus on the mental, emotional, and spiritual aspects of transformation. As we search for connections between yoga and the Twelve Steps, we are much more interested in examining these particular branches.

The term *yoga* is derived from a Sanskrit word meaning "to yoke" and has come to imply "union." It is the name used in India for the transformation of consciousness. Basically, yoga refers to the yoking, joining together, or union of the individual self with the Divine Self, or Higher Power. In a technical sense, yoga also refers to the entire field of techniques and philosophy that has been developed and used for spiritual transformation in India over the past three thousand years. Or we might say that it is the group of methods whose principal purpose is to effect a liberation from separate, or egoic, consciousness.

Nor does yoga refer only to practices used in India; it also includes those renditions which spread to China, Japan, and Tibet. In fact, it makes sense to broaden our concept of yoga to mean "spiritual practice" in general, especially those which aim at ego reduction and subsequent union with the Higher Power. With this understanding, we can say that all spiritual systems, including Christianity, Judaism, Sufism, and others, are yogas. We can relate most readily to this all-inclusive definition as we seek to find the Twelve Steps' place alongside these world systems.

It is also fascinating that two great Indian philosophers used concepts that we can well understand today. Patanjali, one of the most famous of Indian teachers and the formulator of raja yoga, said that yoga is the coming into "contact" with one's own god through powerful personal practice. And Sri Aurobindo, whom we mentioned in the last chapter, stated that "the contact of the human and individual consciousness with the Divine is the very essence of yoga. . . ." These two definitions are remarkably similar to the Eleventh Step and help immeasurably to dispel our doubts that yoga is irrelevant to our own practice.

Through the course of our journey, a dual trajectory has begun to emerge. We have always known that recovery dealt with relationship—to self, others, and the Higher Power. In addition, we are beginning to see that the program ultimately promises us experiences of oneness and identity. For the most part, however, we have tended to focus on the part of Twelve Step practice which maintains the worldview that we are separate individuals. In general, we have not even considered the possibility that a real experience of oneness actually exists, let alone that the Steps could be instrumental in making such a new worldview a reality.

That the Steps *can* do this, and were, in fact, always *meant* to, marks the point where the program becomes a true yoga. If the Steps addressed the issue of relationship only, then we would have to say that as a practice, they were just a forerunner, or a preparatory stage, for the ultimate journey toward wholeness. We hope we have so far demonstrated that they are something more than this. The Twelve Steps do not just take us to the door of the temple. They lead us all the way into the "holy of holies," which is for us a complete change of consciousness that includes oneness with everything as well as separate individuality.

There is a fascinating metaphor characterizing spiritual disciplines that comes from three separate modern sources. As strange as it may seem at first glance, each of these refers to transformational practice as a "technology." Transpersonal theorist Roger Walsh talks about the "technology of transcendence." He is pointing to the central yogic theme of rising above, or transcending, the ego to become one with the true Self, the One, or the Higher Power. He says that at some point we will ultimately be confronted with the question, What is this 'self,' or 'I,' that is in relationship to self, others, and the Higher Power?

Similarly, Grof calls the process of deep self-exploration the "technology of consciousness." According to consciousness research, transformation entails the evolution of our awareness or consciousness. From this perspective, we are led to wonder, What is consciousness itself? What is the relationship between who we think we are and what we are conscious of? Are we ourselves consciousness? These questions are not just idle parlor games we might play to satisfy mere intellectual curiosity. Bill W. said that "deep down in every man, woman, and child is the fundamental idea of God." He called this truth the "Great Reality." As human beings, it is our right to ask such questions. And if what Bill W. and many others seekers of the world say is true, then the answer must also be within us, waiting to be revealed by our Higher Power.

Modern author Georg Feuerstein's fine book on the philosophy of India is entitled *Yoga—The Technology of Ecstasy*. We have already discussed the concept of *ananda*, or ecstasy, as a fundamental characteristic of existence. If we were to follow this logic, we would be quite accurate in referring to the Twelve Steps as the "technology of becoming happy, joyous, and free." It is becoming more and more apparent to us that the goals of yoga, the Twelve Steps, and all true spiritual practices are one and the same.

How, then, should we best proceed in our exploration of yoga?

It is no doubt impossible to attempt an in-depth critique of even one of the many aspects of this profound system. To do so would be a yoga of a lifetime, in and of itself. But perhaps we can briefly outline six principal branches of yoga and highlight those aspects which are directly applicable to Twelve Step practice. For those who feel drawn to more extensive exploration of yoga as an enhancer of Twelve Step practice, we have provided other references in the Bibliography.

Admittedly, to limit the incredibly wide array of Indian yogas into six types is an inherently arbitrary gesture. However, many agree that most disciplines fall somewhere within these classifications. The six we will explore are *jnana*, *bhakti*, *karma*, *raja*, *hatha*, and *mantra*. Let's take a look at each of these to see how they relate to Twelve Step practice.

JNANA YOGA

Jnana yoga uses primarily the *mental* faculties to achieve its goal of union. It is a philosophy and practice of knowledge, insight, and wisdom. Basically, the purpose of jnana yoga is to discern what is considered "real" from what is thought to be "unreal." According to this yoga, identity with the ego self or the body alone is considered unreal. Moreover, identifying exclusively with any separate part, even something as expanded as an archetype, is ultimately considered unreal. Only identity with the true Self, which is none other than the Higher Power, is considered real.

All techniques of jnana yoga are designed to aid seekers in dis-identifying with the unreal aspects of who they are. In accomplishing this task, willpower, aligned with the Divine Will, and inspired reason are considered primary tools. These tools are used in four principal ways: discrimination, renunciation, the cultivation of the spiritual impulse, and the six accomplishments. The six accomplishments are tranquility, self-restraint, abstention, endurance, concentration, and faith.

If we meditate for a moment on these characteristics, it is clear that the Twelve Steps contain many of the principles of jnana yoga. Just as in jnana yoga, sophisticated psychological discrimination is one of the primary components of recovery practice. Throughout the texts, we are asked to use our will, aligned with the Higher Power, and the refined capacities of our intellect in order to make the Steps come alive for us in our lives.

The first, and most important, "unreal" association we must all discern is our false identification with our addiction, or the addicted self. Through Step One, we come to understand, as well as experience, powerlessness and unmanageability. In Step Two, we become able to discriminate between sanity and insanity. And in Step Three, we are required to "make a *decision*," using willingness and the power of our minds to open to the path of surrender.

The next practice of jnana yoga we undertake turns out to be the work of a lifetime. In this stage, we gradually dis-identify with our egos and subsequently begin to identify with our true self as part of the Higher Power. Through the practice of the Fourth and Fifth Steps, we come to understand that a life dominated by character defects is ultimately false, or, as jnana yogis would say, "unreal." Steps Eight and Nine require us to determine, with as much clarity as we can, an appropriate course of reparation. And the Tenth daily demands that we discriminate between right action, or unselfishness, and our egoic, self-centered, or unreal motives on a daily basis.

Many of the promises speak of "understanding" and "coming to know." One of the most important fruits of our practice is a pristine mental clarity that emerges from the fog of confusion created by our active addictions. We are continually confronted with choices between what supports our growth—what leads us toward our real self—and what reinforces our addiction—what can lead us back to our unreal addicted self. We gradually discern that some stories we entertain about ourselves are unreal. And as our willingness to surrender deepens, we replace these with more fulfilling, or real, appraisals.

In recovery circles, we speak constantly about addictive denial and about obsession. If we either are in denial or are obsessed with the thought of our addiction, it is impossible to distinguish between impulses coming from our addiction and from our Higher Power, or between the real and the unreal. These are problems that exist in our *minds*. Only abstinence, and continued reliance on the Higher Power through the Steps, can give us the mental clarity sufficient to discern the real from the unreal. In these very important ways do the Steps fulfill the aims of jnana yoga.

BHAKTI YOGA

Whereas jnana yoga uses the mind as its vehicle for transformation, bhakti yoga focuses primarily on the *emotional nature*. It is often called the yoga of love and devotion. Its aim is to transform the feelings of seekers into a powerful force dedicated to the spiritual search. One text refers to bhakti yoga as "supreme attachment" to the Higher Power. Its Sanskrit root is *bhaj*, which means "to share, or participate in." Using this definition, we could say that recovery is about transforming our attachment or addiction to a substance into the pursuit of spirituality or the Higher Power.

According to ancient texts, there are certain variations of bhakti yoga that a seeker may experience, such as listening, chanting, remembrance, service, ritual, prostration, devotion, friendship, and surrender. Although some of these elements may seem quite foreign, many of them could have been taken right out of any good text on recovery. And of all these, the one most referred to by practitioners of bhakti yoga is surrender of self to the Divine, or Higher Power. For this reason alone we could say that the Steps are a form of bhakti yoga.

There are also other fascinating aspects of this branch of yoga that have implications for us in recovery. For example, bhakti yoga does not aim at the eradication of passion, as do many other yogas. Instead, its practitioners strive to redirect this passion into a more appropriate use of it. They do not seek to get rid of desire, but to transform or channel it into the desire for the Higher Power alone.

The Big Book also proposes such a transmuting of passion in

its discussion of the troublesome aspects of sexuality. We are told that in order to quiet the imperious urge, we should "throw ourselves the harder into helping others." This refocusing of problematic emotional states is exactly the type of service to which the scriptures of bhakti yoga are referring. In a sense, the ancients saw the archetypal nature of Emotion as neither bad nor good, but rather as a powerful force that could be harnessed for spiritual growth instead of being wasted in the destructive pursuit of addiction.

In a similar vein, practitioners of bhakti yoga frequently refer to "God intoxication." Many of the greatest poets of the East, such as Omar Khayyam, Rumi, Kabir, and Tukaram, were themselves bhakti yogis. In their poems, they frequently spoke of drunkenness. But if we read between the lines, this intoxication is referring to an intense, ecstatic love for the Higher Power that consumes the emotions of the seeker and transforms them into one all-encompassing passion for conscious contact.

Bill W. said of his spiritual experience, "I knew that I was loved and could love in return." Through the grace of surrender, many of us begin for the first time to learn what real love actually is. This love manifests itself in the fellowships and spreads to include all our relationships. Ultimately, as we seek to improve our conscious contact, we are given the gift of an ever-widening feeling of devotion to our Higher Power. The closer our conscious contact becomes, the more we are able to experience this power of love and devotion. These go hand in hand with an ever-deepening sense of humility, and a more wholehearted readiness to allow our Higher Power to transform us.

Other texts of bhakti yoga refer to four movements of the discipline. These are the desire of the soul for God, the pain of love and the return of love from the Divine, the delight of love, and the eternal enjoyment of being the lover of the Higher Power. As we move toward wholeness, what better way to celebrate the power of our emotions than to surrender them into one great emotion of love for the Higher Power? This is the promise of bhakti yoga and one of the promises of deep Twelve Step practice as well. It is what Bill W. called the "language of the heart."

KARMA YOGA

Thus far, we have outlined yogas that deal with the mind and the emotions. The word *karma* comes from the Sanskrit root *kri*, meaning "make" or "do." Karma yoga, then, is a yoga of *action* and uses as its main force the power of *will*. Whereas bhakti yoga concerns itself with the channeling of emotions toward the Higher Power, karma yoga is a strategy that enables the practitioner to dedicate the results of action and works to the Divine.

One of the principal expositions of karma yoga is in the famous Indian work the *Bhagavad Gita*, or *Song of God*. In this narrative, the Higher Power, in the form of Krishna, teaches his student, Arjuna, about the nature of existence and the ways to improve conscious contact with the Divine. Krishna explains that one of the surest means to accomplish this is through service and the dedication of all one's actions to the Higher Power.

The *Bhagavad Gita* distinguishes between several types of actions. First, there is wrong, or harmful action, which results in negative consequences for the "doer." Then, there are right, or helpful, works, which benefit others and which bring positive results to the doer. Although these are obviously more advantageous than harmful actions, Krishna says that they are still not the best form of works. This is because there is still some selfish motive involved in the action. The doer still desires to experience the fruits of the labor.

However, there is one other form of work that is considered more correct than either of the other two. This is action performed in which the doer surrenders the fruits of the work to the Higher Power and gives up the need to experience any benefit or return from them. We discussed this same principle in the last chapter when we described the process of surrendering up the need to be the "doer" altogether. By surrendering the fruits of our good actions, our separate ego self dissolves into the Higher Power and we are freed of the bonds of isolation.

In light of these characteristics of karma yoga, the Twelfth Step immediately comes to mind. "Service" and "carrying the message" are cornerstones of the program. Every recovery text extols the need for *action* and for right use of will, or alignment with the will of the Higher Power. The Twelve Steps are probably more aligned with karma yoga than with any other form. But karma yoga's differentiation between the various types of right action really requires us to examine how we practice our own Twelfth Step.

Program pioneers definitely exercised forethought in the way they worded AA's final Step. It is clear that we do Twelfth Step work not because we are saints, but because we want to stay sober. It is part of *our* program, not of the one with whom we are working. Presenting the concept of service in this way is a wise safeguard against our rampant egos. We just could not handle thinking we were special because of the work we do for others.

But we hope that how we work the Twelfth Step will evolve in such a way that our worldview gradually changes as the result of practicing the Steps. Eventually, we may be able to perform this Step in the spirit of self-surrender, or as a channel for the Higher Power's energy, as the Prayer of St. Francis describes. We might find ourselves giving up the need to be special. And ultimately, if the yogas of the world are right, we may find that we are almost out of the picture altogether and that the Higher Power is actually the doer of our good works. This is the place where the Twelve Steps fulfill the role of karma yoga.

RAJA YOGA

As we mentioned, raja yoga is the discipline outlined in the work of Patanjali, known as the *Yoga Sutras*. It is sometimes called the "royal yoga," or the "yoga of kings," and is often considered the most rigorous and intense of all the yogas. A *sutra* is a short phrase that was used in ancient India as a teaching format. In his *Yoga Sutras*, Patanjali spelled out an elaborate system of mental, physical, and emotional training that resulted in various changes of consciousness.

In the West, the discipline that most closely resembles raja yoga is consciousness research. Basically, this royal yoga consists of techniques to access what consciousness researchers call "non-ordinary" states of consciousness. Non-ordinary states are those in which consciousness is not limited to the body or the ego, or to linear time. For our purposes, raja yoga corresponds to the Eleventh Step and all the methods we use to seek to improve our conscious contact with the Higher Power.

Some of the techniques involve the use of the breath in much the same way as the breathwork we explained in other chapters. In India, some of these were called *pranayama*. Other disciplines deal with the awakening of the spiritual force that mystics have said lies dormant within all individuals. This is that energy we also described in the last chapter, and which we said ultimately results in the state of ecstasy. Patanjali also outlined many methods of concentration and meditation, as well as techniques of moral purification, which are required in order for the seeker to utilize deep experiential methods.

Our normal understanding of the Eleventh Step concerns the improvement of our "conscious contact." Our newest interpretation focuses on "consciousness" itself, and how it changes as we use prayer, meditation, and other Eleventh Step methods. The goal of yoga *includes* conscious contact, but goes beyond this to mean "union," or the point where contact becomes identity. This particular horizon of the Eleventh Step marks the crossroads where the Twelve Steps meet the requirements of a yoga.

HATHA YOGA

Hatha yoga is primarily the yoga of the *physical body*. It is sometimes called the "forceful yoga" and has as its goal the same aim as the rest of the yogas: the union of the individual self with the Higher Power. Many ancient sources point out that the body goes through just as many intense changes on the road to union as do the emotions and the mind. Therefore, hatha yoga was developed as a way to prepare the body for these transformations that come about due to spiritual awakening.

Although practices working with the body are also a part of other yogas, particularly raja yoga, they are primarily the domain of hatha yoga. This form relies on a rigorous regime of *asanas*, or postures, which, when consistently practiced, bring about the purification of the body and a freeing of the energy that is ordinarily latent within the system.

The development of body-oriented therapies in the humanistic era of psychology marks the point where the basic principle of hatha yoga began to be introduced into the Western mainstream. Since that time, the number of different forms of bodywork has greatly increased. Now there is a wide variety from which to choose—not just from hatha yoga, but from many world sources. As we mentioned in chapter 6, "The Treasure Trove," we have not paid a great deal of attention to the health of the body. Fortunately, this situation has begun to change in the past few decades, so that now body-oriented therapies are much more prevalent in addictions and codependence treatment.

Still, many recovery seekers report that when it comes to their program, they are most often neglectful of the body's recovery. Since specific techniques for freeing the body from its share of the ravages of addiction are not specifically addressed in the basic texts, we can place hatha yoga, and other forms of practice focusing on the body, in the ranks of Eleventh Step methods. Thankfully, this is an area of transformation that is gaining more respect and attention as seekers continue to expand the definitions and possibilities of recovery.

MANTRA YOGA

The word *mantra*, which comes from the Sanskrit word meaning "man" and "to think," or from *manas*, meaning "mind." This is the science of sound and sound repetition. The ancients believed not only that the meaning of words was important, but also that the arrangement of syllables and the sound they make when spoken had the power to change consciousness. Therefore, they developed a yoga based on the repetition of various words and syllables, each of which performed a particular function in terms of aiding the seeker to improve conscious contact.

In India, practitioners referred to these phrases as *mantras*. In the Sufi tradition of Moslem cultures, they were called *wazifas*. Mantras were derived from Sanskrit, whereas wazifas had their roots in ancient Aramaic. Traditionally, a mantra was transmitted from an *adept*, or teacher, to a student, who then repeated the mantra silently or out loud, in meditation or throughout daily activities. According to mystics, the repetition of the sounds somehow created a resonant vibration with certain energies of the Higher Power, which could then bring about transformation.

Many seekers report being turned off by the way mantra yoga has been marketed in the West over the past few decades. But this hybrid popularization notwithstanding, mantra yoga is a highly respected form of spiritual practice worldwide. One of its most accessible forms has been singing and chanting. Either done individually or in groups, these renditions have been praised by many seekers as being enhancers of psychological and spiritual growth.

The program makes no claim that its slogans can alter consciousness by the power of the English syllables themselves. However, thousands of seekers report that the repetition of the sayings, Steps, Serenity Prayer, and wisdom "sutras" heard daily in meetings is a vital component of recovery. In this way we have always practiced our own brand of mantra yoga. As more practitioners discover the treasure trove of world methods, taking on any of the sciences that include chanting, singing, or repetition of phrases should not be too foreign an undertaking.

THE INTEGRAL YOGA OF SRI AUROBINDO

Although most yogas are millennia old, there have been a few important developments in this domain in recent times. Probably the most powerful of these in the twentieth century has been the contribution of the famous Indian philosopher-mystic, Sri Aurobindo. Aurobindo took up the threads of all the great yogas and wove them into a synthesis that he called "integral yoga." In addition, he used some refreshingly original definitions of yoga as a foundation for his synthesis. These definitions, and the principles of integral yoga itself, are remarkably applicable to the Western mind in general, and to us in recovery in particular.

Aurobindo taught that not only do humans evolve toward perfection, but that all of life and creation move toward some goal of completion. According to him, this movement has two trajectories. The first is "involution," or the era where the perfection and unity of the Divine involves itself in the myriad and separate manifestations of creation. The second part is "evolution," where the One, which has played all the roles of separate creation, evolves back into the unity of itself.

If this is true, then in a sense, all life is a yoga, because the whole thrust of creation is a return to a union with the Divine. This is the same process we humans undergo in our spiritual journey. The only difference is that for humans, yoga *condenses*, into a shortened time frame and an intense practice, the normal long evolution of creation back to the Source.

Have you ever noticed how your growth has been speeded up by the process of the Steps? Have you also become aware that when you took on an Eleventh Step method, that rapid evolution was accelerated even more? It seems to make a lot of sense that what our Higher power is accomplishing for us is just a crash course in the natural evolution of all of creation back to its original state of unity.

Aurobindo called his integral yoga the "triple path of works, love, and knowledge." In his masterful treatise entitled *The Synthesis of Yoga*, he demonstrated how three branches of classic Indian yoga—karma, bhakti, and jnana—could be combined into one unified practice. Aurobindo asserted that it was important to engage all three aspects of the human being: the body, through the process of will and action; the mind; and the emotions. He believed that this represented the flowering of India's yogas for the twentieth century and beyond.

Aurobindo's work has an uncanny relevance for recovery seekers. In a very real sense, *Twelve Step practice is itself an integral yoga*. It definitely combines the philosophy of bhakti, jnana, and karma yoga. It is without question a triple path of love, knowledge, and works. It begins with surrender, proceeds through sophisticated psychological discrimination, and culminates in service to others.

In previous chapters we have traced the lineage of the Twelve Steps in the same way that practitioners of other yogas have traced their heritage back to the roots of their particular disciplines. Although it does not seem likely that Sri Aurobindo's work is actually part of the foundation of the Twelve Steps, it is difficult to imagine that it does not somehow belong to the recovery lineage, at least in spirit. Aurobindo wrote at length about the importance of surrender and even spoke frequently of the Divine as the Higher Power.

The final part of the Twelfth Step admonishes us "to practice these principles in all our affairs." We eventually discover that the program does not have a spiritual "part." *The entire program is spiritual.* There is not one thing that we can separate out from the rest of our practice and say that it does not fall under the domain of spirituality.

Modern teacher Ram Dass wrote a book entitled *Grist for the Mill.* He said that *everything* we do is grist for the mill of our own awakening. If we can be aware, or conscious, of our emotional and psychological reactions to the various acts we perform daily, each act can be an opportunity to clear ourselves of some past pattern. As the patterns emerge, we use the Steps to deal with them, particularly Steps One through Three and Steps Six and Seven.

For example, we can practice "highway yoga" or "grocery store yoga." In each of these circumstances, we can learn an enormous amount about ourselves if we can be as conscious as we can of what comes up for us. This is what we mean about the Steps' being a yoga. It is also what Aurobindo meant when he said, "All life is yoga."

THE STEPDANCE

There are many beautiful poetic metaphors that world cultures have for the nature of the universe. For example, in India, creation is often referred to as a *lila*, or the "divine play." According to this description, the Divine, in its original oneness, is manifested as all the multiple aspects of one great drama. Another variation on this theme is that the archetypes of Chance or Infinite Possibility ensure that the drama is not predetermined, but that each of us, as an individual part of the Divine and an actor in the play, has free will. Still others highlight more the "play" aspect of the drama, while holding out the possibility of transcending the suffering inherent in existence.

From another perspective, the universe is described as a great dance. It is said to be the dance of various gods and goddesses who are representations of the Higher Power, from Krishna, to Kali, to Shiva. Ram Dass helped to popularize this metaphor in the West with his book *The Only Dance There Is*.

When I was little, I took dancing lessons. The first thing we were shown was the *steps* to the dance. We first learned them with our minds. Next, we slowly walked through the steps, a little at a time, until we began to feel more comfortable with them. At this stage, the halting moves we made bore little resemblance to the grace and fluidity with which our teacher performed the dance.

After a while, we began to get the feel of them. At this point we did not have to be always thinking about them. Instead we found that our bodies somehow knew what to do automatically. As our fears lessened, our skills grew, until more and more the steps became second nature to us.

Finally, we realized that the knowledge of the steps had deepened beyond our intellects and was an intimate part of ourselves. At that point, we were ready to let go completely and let the intuitive grace of our bodies and the natural flow of artistic creativity take over. We had learned to dance.

This is precisely how we have come to experience the Twelve Steps. In the beginning, they seemed more like foreign precepts, almost like the Ten Commandments. At first, we put them together in our heads. Gradually, we implemented them and began to experience their benefits in our lives. It felt important to take them and ourselves quite seriously.

But over time, as the Steps become more a part of us, we loosen up a little bit. They seem to exist within us in their entirety as a wholeness in any given moment, waiting to burst forth singly or collectively, as we need them, under the intuitive guidance of the Higher Power. Eventually, it becomes difficult to distinguish ourselves from the Steps and the program. We *are* the practice. This is what the ancients meant by becoming the "Tao," or the Way. The Way is not something outside ourselves. We are ourselves the Way.

Finally, we begin to sense a profound purpose in learning the Steps, beyond that of mere abstinence. Just as some of us learned the steps to our childhood dance, we now realize that the Steps have taken us to the threshold of a great Dance too. All our years of faltering practice—first taking baby steps and gradually becoming more surefooted—have been a preparation for this moment. Now is the time to take the leap and join the dance. We will no longer have to rely on our minds, but will instead be guided by the grace and creativity of our Higher Power from within our own hearts.

This, then, is the Stepdance. We have proceeded slowly until we have known the Steps with our hearts. But we have not learned them only to stand by and be forever separate from the rest of creation. We have learned them so that we can dance. They have taken us to the brink of the great Mystery—the place where the Steps become the universal Dance. The purpose of the Steps has always been to teach us to be dancers. The ultimate promise of surrender is that we no longer need to hold ourselves back from the fullness of life. Instead, we can now let go and join the Dance.

CHAPTER TEN

Recovery as Tao—How This Way Works

> *The Great Way has no gate;*
> *there are a thousand paths to it.*
>
> —Wu Men
>
> *We have found nothing incompatible between a powerful spiritual experience and a life of sane and happy usefulness.*
>
> —Bill W.

In a sense, "Stepdance" is the end of our journey. For the last nine chapters, we have tried to present the Twelve Steps as a true world discipline. To set the stage for making this vision a reality, we have provided language and structure for a more comprehensive spiritual interpretation of the Steps.

However, there are some important epilogues to this odyssey, which we will cover in these final two chapters. It is time now to reground ourselves in the practical realities of everyday recovery. Our current task is to demonstrate how this perspective can be implemented in the lives of seekers on a daily basis.

In order to do this, we will first go straight to the Steps. How can they cross the boundary between our previous worldview and our new understanding of reality? Somehow, they must apply to the further realms of the psyche if we are even to consider making these dimensions part of our journey. Next, it is time to hear the accounts of a few seekers who have already ventured beyond the crossroads. It should be interesting to find out just what some of their experiences have been, and how these experiences have actually enhanced their recovery. And finally, we will pass on a few strategies that have already helped others in translating spiritual principles into action.

THE STEPS IN OTHER DIMENSIONS

Step One—In chapter 7, "Surrender—The Mystery of Death and Rebirth," we made the point that the experience of powerlessness, followed by surrender, is archetypal to humanity. It is quite common these days to hear the phrase "coming into power" used to refer to a certain stage of psychological and spiritual growth.

Coming into power seems to be particularly important in the experiential work of those dealing with issues of codependence. The surrendering of power to people, places, and things is a primary characteristic of this condition. Therefore, reclaiming this power is a necessary step in the transformational process.

The question then arises, What do we do with this power once we have taken it back? For those of us practicing the Twelve Steps who have experienced the results of the abuse of power in our own lives, this question has a special relevance. How do we reconcile the two philosophies of "coming into power" and an "acceptance of powerlessness"?

If we use the principle of complementarity, that two seemingly contradictory observations can coexist within the same philosophy, as we discussed in chapter 5, "New Maps," then we can say that both these concepts are important. But what is more crucial is the question of timing. From our own experience, and that of world seekers, the most effective thing we can do with the power we take back is to surrender it as soon as we can to the Higher Power.

The fact that we gave it away to begin with implies that we at least had the right idea. We have always been meant to surrender personal power. However, instead of giving it away to people, places, and things, we are required to surrender it to the Higher Power. The irony of continually surrendering any power accrued to us is that it will be returned by the Higher Power in an even greater measure than when we gave it.

This reciprocal dynamic that we are engaged in with the

Higher Power—surrendering power and being graced with a fuller dispensation of it—is the expanded action of the First and Third Steps across the boundaries of our old worldview and on into our newfound perspective. No matter what stage of spiritual development we may find ourselves in, *the First Step will always be the foundation*. Our own experience, and world traditions, tell us that the ego is just too subtle and pervasive for us to assume that it can handle any degree of power for its own use.

The yoga of the First and Third Steps allows for every gift of power to be returned to its source, in full faith that we will again receive the grace of power sufficient to carry out our Higher Power's will. After all, what we pray for in the Eleventh Step is to *know* what we are supposed to do, and to be given the *power* to carry it out. Thus, this action brings together the First, Third, and Eleventh Steps in a wonderful synergy that daily supports our ultimate goal of the ego death followed by oneness with the Higher Power.

Step Two—As we proceed on our journey, we will discover that the Second Step also continues to be a vital dynamic in recovery. But as our consciousness of ourselves, the Higher Power, and the universe expands through practice of the Eleventh Step, we may come to realize that our definition of sanity itself also undergoes a transformation.

According to basic Freudian psychology, sanity may be defined as being oriented in the Newtonian-Cartesian paradigm, or the worldview that says human beings are forever separate objects in a mechanistic universe. Freud also said that the goal of psychoanalysis is to restore human beings who are in great suffering to the condition of "normal" everyday suffering. These are fairly pessimistic appraisals of human potential.

It is even more profoundly perplexing that the whole of Western civilization has for the most part subscribed to this worldview as well. And it is this type of thinking that is largely responsible for many of the crises that threaten the survival of life on this planet today. In our cultural egocentricity, we tend to discount native and aboriginal cultures as being primitive and uncivilized. But from their point of view, a society like our own whose voracious lifestyle may actually destroy the very planet on which we all live is the one which is truly insane.

Pioneers of transpersonal psychology recognized that there is a form of "lower" and "higher" sanity. Lower sanity enables human beings to function in the everyday world. But higher sanity lets us see ourselves in a radically different way. Rather than seeing ourselves as separate objects, we come to experience our connectedness and oneness with others, with the Higher Power, and with nature and the universe at large.

With this alternate perspective, it is impossible to continue those behaviors which are harmful to others and the environment, because *we ourselves are "others and the environment."* Practitioners of deep Eleventh Step methods report that they too have reached similar conclusions. They find that the Higher Power is gradually restoring them to greater and greater levels of sanity.

However, what is sanity in one era of our lives may not be wholly sane for another. Once we begin to see our world differently, we may perhaps find that our approach toward life has been insane in other ways. At these times, we can turn once more to the Steps—and to the Second in particular—and allow ourselves to be restored again to a more expanded awareness of sanity.

Step Three—In "Surrender—The Mystery of Death and Rebirth," we also stretched the limits of surrender and the Third Step. As one of the goals of deep Twelve Step work, we proposed the possibility of living in the moment-to-moment process of surrender. Our need to make a decision in as complete a way as possible should never change, and will always be a cornerstone of our practice. But if this does not change as we go deeper into the mystery of the Third Step, then what does?

The answer to this question is that it is our *awareness* of what we consider our *life* to be that undergoes transformation. Up until now, we have thought our life to be the time from birth to the present. But, as we said once before, we now find that this biographical life is but the *foam* on the surface of a *wave* on the surface of an *ocean* of existence. Therefore, because our life includes more and more, in a sense we are required to surrender more and more.

One of the major pitfalls on the spiritual journey is that we sometimes think we are getting more spiritual, only to discover that our egos are actually getting bigger and bigger. Almost every spiritual discipline includes practices that are safeguards against this "universalizing" of the ego. Since staying sober is our number one priority, any discipline that includes ego deflation is indeed welcome. Again, it is the mysterious reciprocal relationship with the Higher Power that is at the heart of our efforts. We are required to make a decision to surrender every aspect of our newly expanded life experience. Yet we receive in return the gift of life in a richer measure than we could have ever known.

Steps Four and Five—Many seekers say that undergoing Eleventh Step methods has also greatly enhanced their practice of the Fourth and Fifth Steps. In deep experiential work, they are able to make conscious many situations, behaviors, emotions, and motives of which they were previously unaware. But, to continue our current line of thought, they are discovering that their inventory now includes not just biographical information, but also the perinatal and the transpersonal dimensions of the psyche.

Most of us rely on the aid of a trusted guide, sponsor, or therapist to help us understand our deep experiences. Sharing our archetypal, birth, or biographical stories helps to complete the integration process and expands our use of the Fifth Step. Also, seekers report that in the non-ordinary states of consciousness produced by some Eleventh Step methods, they often feel a profound intimacy with the Higher Power. In this space, they have been able to confront and admit the "exact nature of their wrongs" in a more fulfilling way than ever before.

Steps Six and Seven—The Sixth and Seventh Steps have remarkable applications to the journey beyond the crossroads. For the most part, we have used them to continue the cleansing we began in the Fourth and Fifth Steps. However, these Steps take on a much more active role in a Twelve Step yoga. We find that they are vital in the continued daily process of becoming conscious.

In our everyday interaction with others, we often discover that a seemingly insignificant event is a trigger for an emotional reaction that is out of all proportion to the original occurrence.

The reaction occurs when the event has connected with some deep pattern of which we are either partially or entirely unconscious. This is one of the reasons we seek therapy or a spiritual practice.

The first thing we must do is to break up the energetic block created by the pattern, which has accumulated over the years. To accomplish this, we take on any of the deep experiential methods that allow for some form of catharsis. Once the main "charge" has been made conscious and released, we generally feel much freer. However, this does not mean that we have completed the healing process. We will still find ourselves reacting in our everyday lives, though less frequently. But now we should be able to approach these emergences from our psyche differently.

This is where the Sixth and Seventh Steps become important. We have made the point that consciousness, or awareness, is itself a healing power. Therefore, when we become aware that material is emerging from our psyche, our task is to be as conscious as possible of *every reaction* we may have. If we have done a thorough Fourth and Fifth Step, then we probably have some insight into the nature and origin of the pattern that is coming up. As soon as we recognize the pattern, *and even if we do not*, we immediately work the Sixth and Seventh Steps.

We become as "entirely ready" as we can, and then "humbly ask" our Higher Power to remove the emergence. In this way, we are continually working with the healing power of consciousness. We perform the triple action of becoming aware of the pattern, becoming ready to release it, and then surrendering it up to the Higher Power. We can eventually learn to do all this automatically, in any life situation. It is a way that the Steps can be worked as a moment-to-moment yoga. This practice links the Steps with many meditative disciplines of the world. In particular, it is similar to the Buddhist process of mindfulness that we discussed in chapter 6, "The Treasure Trove."

Steps Eight and Nine—Steps Four through Nine are all concerned with clearing away the wreckage of the past. In the Eighth and Ninth Steps, we directly address the issue of personal relationship by making amends. But just as we have learned that our past is much more vast than we had previously realized, we find we can also bring to light our connectedness to a much longer chain of relationships than our current biographical ones.

The term *family of origin* has become quite popular in the codependence movement. From our current observations, we learn that this family of origin includes not just our parents and siblings, but also our entire ancestry. In deep Eleventh Step work, seekers report being able to trace their patterns beyond their biographical family on into their ancestral roots, and even to the place where ancestry merges with national and racial origins. Ultimately, they have found that these patterns belong somehow to humanity at large.

With this type of sweeping perspective, the term *blame* ceases to have any relevant meaning. It is difficult to hold any one person, or group of persons, responsible for our patterns without somehow indicting all of humanity. Although it is possible to reach the place in consciousness where we experience the imperfections of humanity, many seekers report being able to go beyond this to a wholehearted acceptance and compassion for the entire human condition.

Other explorers of deep Twelve Step realms make an additional fascinating observation. They somehow get the feeling that they are healing not just themselves, but also an entire family or cultural pattern. For whatever reason, they experience that the "sins of generations" will no longer be passed on if they can do all they can now to heal those parts of themselves that have participated in the perpetuation of the pattern. In a sense, the buck can stop here.

This hopeful attitude has tremendous implications for the nurturing of the next generation, and ultimately for the future of all humanity. The all-encompassing acceptance of our kinship with the whole of humanity, including the dysfunction that has been passed on since time immemorial, is the natural result of deep Eighth and Ninth Step work. We experience a profound satisfaction in being intimately involved not only in our own transformation, but also in the healing of the whole.

Step Ten—The Tenth Step, one of the "maintenance" Steps, is our invitation to begin truly practicing a daily yoga. One of the goals of deep practice worldwide is to discover, and become, our true self as part of the Higher Power. Steps One through Nine have shown us the power of our false self, or ego, and have provided techniques for freeing us from the character defects that make up this egoic self.

World systems often define our first contact with this real self as the "witness," or the "observer." While we are in denial or under the sway of our addiction or some character defect, for all intents and purposes we *are* the defect. But at some point, we become *aware*, or *conscious*, of the fact of the defect. This unit of consciousness that stands apart from the pattern and is capable of observing it is what we call the witness. It is also the beginning of the true self.

Becoming aware that we are at least sometimes the witness of our patterns is a signal that we are truly in the transformational process. It is a fact that if we experience ourselves as the witness of something, then we cannot *be* the thing we are witnessing. This means that we are *free*, at least for the time being, of the power of the pattern. The freeing up of consciousness from the power of our addictions and defects is one way to characterize the entire healing adventure.

Remember that we have frequently repeated how consciousness itself is a healing power. The witness self is the agent of consciousness that we use to make the healing process a daily reality. Every moment that we are able to observe a pattern, we are freeing ourselves from its power. If we have done a thorough job with Steps Four through Nine, then we have already released many of the blocks we have been accumulating throughout our lives. Consequently, it should be easier for us to be the witness and not "get caught" as often as we once did in our patterns and dysfunctional behaviors.

Here is how the witness works: I lose my temper. At this point, "I am angry," or "*I am the anger.*" All of a sudden, I become *aware* that I am angry. At this moment, I am *not* the anger. *I am the witness of the anger.* I watch myself be angry. I may be thinking, "Ah, look at me being angry." And I soon realize that as long as I am observing the anger, it does not have a paralyzing hold on me. I am in fact watching and allowing the anger to emerge, flow through me, and be surrendered up to the

Higher Power, just as we all have done in many of the Eleventh Step methods. I might also discover that unless I have already done some good release work in letting go of the anger, it is impossible to be the fair witness.

This is the healing process in action. It is a way to bring the power of Eleventh Step methods into a moment-to-moment daily practice. To stand back and observe our behavior, and to "promptly admit it" when we are wrong, depends on our ability to be a fair witness of our actions. We gradually realize that this witness of our behavior is the true self that continually seeks to improve its conscious contact and, ultimately, its identity, with the Higher Power.

Step Eleven—Since we have already gone to such lengths in other chapters to focus on the power of the Eleventh Step, we do not need to spend much time here reiterating its importance. By now we should realize that improving conscious contact into the dimensions of oneness and identity is at the heart of deep Twelve Step work. All the Steps are concerned with a change of consciousness, and nowhere is this change made more explicit than in the Eleventh Step.

Step Twelve—The Twelfth Step is our rendition of karma yoga in action. Our introduction to the concept of service comes, for most of us, from our interactions with our groups. This dynamic of service finds its first fulfillment in the final Step, when we seek to give away what has been given to us and to carry the message to other suffering addicts. But many world traditions have a similar "step," which actually carries the concept of service to an even more fulfilling conclusion.

One of the greatest examples of these is the archetype of the *Bodhisattva* in India. *Bodhisattva* means "compassionate one." A person who realizes oneness with the Higher Power but chooses to stay in the world of separation until every person reaches that same state of consciousness is called a Bodhisattva. In a sense, Bodhisattvas surrender up their bliss and choose to serve all of humanity, even if it means they must continue to suffer themselves. They realize that the purpose of their own enlightenment is not to selfishly enjoy being happy, joyous, and free, but to carry the message of freedom to all sufferers everywhere.

One of the greatest gifts of Twelve Step practice is our realization that we are citizens of the world, or part of humanity. We are not just addicts or codependents, but *beings* whose identity includes the Higher Power and even the entire universe. If we translate the Twelfth Step into a larger dimension, we may perhaps discover that our newest spiritual awakening requires us to serve not just addicts, but humanity and all of creation as well. Then, as we practice these principles in all our affairs, we can truly say that we are working a Twelve Step yoga.

ADVENTURES

Reading actual accounts of seekers' adventures beyond the crossroads can help make philosophy a reality. It personalizes this journey in a way no amount of theorizing can accomplish. Here, then, are three such stories, which should demonstrate how deep Eleventh Step work enhances our Twelve Step practice. The names used are fictitious and the wording has been paraphrased from the three seekers' reports.

ROBERT'S STORY—FINDING THE MOTHER

Robert is a recovering alcoholic, as well as an adult child of an alcoholic. Much of the focus of his codependence work has been about resolving his issues with his mother. Before this account took place, he had undergone various forms of traditional and nontraditional therapy. His mother had also been through treatment and additional therapy as part of her own recovery from alcoholism. Although they had attended a therapy session together, Robert felt that for them to try to work out their issues face-to-face would be just too traumatic for him. He subscribed to the accepted doctrine that he could not be healed until he had faced the trauma of his family of origin. For this reason, he often shamed himself, and he nearly despaired of ever finding freedom.

At a deeply experiential intensive, Robert participated in a creative visualization, or guided imagery session. During the visualization, he experienced being visited by Mary, the mother of Christ. He reports that Mary told him that she would be his mother from that point on. She also said that as the archetype of Motherhood, she would be the inner guide of his meditation and deep experiential work.

Robert recounts that for the first time in his life, he understood what it was like to be loved with a mother's love. From then on, there was a sense of nurturing, safety, and trust inside him that he had never known before. In addition, he began to have all sorts of insights about his relationship with his mother.

Robert realized that he had been expecting his mother to do something for him that *no person, place, or thing on earth* could ever possibly do, much less his own mother. What he wanted was to be absolutely loved, and to feel okay about himself. But he had wanted *her* to do this for *him*. Having had the experience of Mary's giving him unconditional acceptance, he understood that this type of nurturing must come from within himself. Nothing outside of him could ever accomplish it.

Robert knew that he had not had a "visitation" from Mary. But he believed that the way his Higher Power chose to heal him was to give him an experience of the archetype of Motherhood. It was the Higher Power within him who was the healer, in the form of the Divine Mother. By finding that love within himself, Robert freed his mother from having to meet those impossible expectations that he previously had of her. As a result of seeing her in this new light, their relationship began to change. Although they continue to have their ups and downs, Robert says that he has never been the same since that experience. Now he *knows* that there is a source of real love deep inside him, brought to him by the Higher Power in the form of the Divine Mother.

Robert's story demonstrates some remarkable qualities of deep Eleventh Step work. First, it shows how transpersonal experiences, such as confrontation with the Great Mother archetype, can be instrumental in biographical healing. And second, it demonstrates once more how our inner healer, or Higher Power, is in charge of our therapeutic process. In hindsight, his resistance to traditional therapy was but a prelude to the more personally appropriate form of therapeutic work his inner healer had in store for him. We cannot possibly *know* what form our healing will take. But if we open to all the possibilities of transformation, including what the further reaches of the psyche may divulge, we will, in the final analysis, have a much greater opportunity to experience wholeness.

DEBBIE'S STORY—CODEPENDENCE AND THE PERINATAL

Debbie is a young woman who recently completed codependence treatment. Among the many issues she explored while in treatment were her sense of always feeling responsible for other people and her inability to establish boundaries between herself and others, especially her family of origin. Back in her hometown, she attended a breathwork intensive to enhance her recovery.

During her session, Debbie experienced her own birth, from the womb, through the canal, and into delivery. She reports that as the fetus in the womb, she was able to feel her mother's emotions as her own. She was later able to verify this by discussing the pregnancy with her mother. After the birth process had begun, she remembered having the consciousness of the fetus, or the one being born, as well as the consciousness of the mother, or the one giving birth.

Debbie relates that when she was in the consciousness of being her mother, she experienced agonizing pain. And when she was herself, as the fetus, she realized that at some very primary level, she felt responsible for her mother's suffering. In addition, she experienced the trauma of being suffocated in the birth canal and needing to free herself physically from her mother just to stay alive. As she relived coming into the delivery room, Debbie recalls feeling smothered, as though her mother were "all over her." This sense of psychological suffocation, which was so strong as to be almost physical, she remembers having had almost her whole life.

After the birthing experience, Debbie reported that she truly belonged to herself for the first time in her life. She finally understood where much of her misplaced sense of responsibility had originated. She also had the insight that the struggle in the birth canal, where the consciousness of the mother and fetus is often undifferentiated, was a cause of her inability to maintain boundaries between herself and others. Even though she had worked on her rage in treatment, it was not until she experienced her birth that she truly began to find freedom from her codependence.

DENNIS'S STORY—ANOTHER FIRST STEP EXPERIENCE

Dennis is a recovering alcoholic who attended a month-long seminar on transpersonal aspects of addiction. Dennis said that for the first three weeks, it felt like addictions treatment. In all his experiential sessions he was facing powerlessness, yet was consistently unable to surrender. He felt hopeless and stuck. Somehow, he knew he was going through an ego death, but he just did not believe he would ever complete it.

In one of his final experiential sessions, Dennis found himself right back in the familiar territory of hopelessness. He recalls that while in the non-ordinary state of consciousness, he was in a place filled with lepers, beggars, and many other people in terrible suffering. Although they aroused in him feelings of disgust, he somehow identified with them. This was accompanied by a more profound sense of shame than he had felt at any other time in his life.

He wept, struggled, and prayed repeatedly to get out of that place. Finally, it dawned on him that he was going to be in this leper's hell for eternity and that he was powerless to get out. He began to accept the unacceptable. He decided that if he was going to be there forever, then he might as well make himself useful. At that thought, a silver bowl filled with clear water and some white linen cloths appeared. Dennis took up the cloths and began to clean the lepers' sores.

In that instant, an image of a smiling Mother Teresa appeared, and together they began to work with the beggars. Immediately, the scene shifted, and Dennis realized that he was no longer in hell. He was free! He understood that he had finally accepted powerlessness on a very deep level and had been given the grace of surrender. Yet, somehow he knew the journey was not yet over.

In the next moment, he found himself at the foot of a vast set of steps that led up to a beautiful temple on the summit of a hill. Dennis remembered getting very excited at this point. He had heard and read stories of "initiations" and "illuminations," where seekers were filled with light and glory. He felt that this must be his time! So he started to ascend the stairs, figuring that there must be a pedestal or throne room somewhere up there with his name on it.

All of a sudden, two monks dressed in simple brown robes appeared at the bottom of the stairs. He realized that they were smiling and holding brooms. They gazed at him gently and then went on about their business of sweeping the foot of the stairs. Dennis said that, at last, he "got it." Instead of climbing the stairs and then ascending the throne of his personal glorification, his job was to serve—just as he and Mother Teresa had done in the lepers' hell, and just as these two monks were doing now. So he picked up a broom and began to sweep the steps along with them.

At that moment, he realized that he had truly experienced surrender. His struggle was over. It had been his ego's desire to sit on the throne. But when he was able to find peace in just sweeping around beneath the throne, he knew that he had undergone some form of the ego death.

After the session, Dennis remembers that everything seemed different. He said he felt like a newborn baby. He no longer needed to struggle to "get through" anything. He called this the truest feeling of surrender that he had ever experienced. He finally knew what the Big Book was talking about.

A DAY IN THE LIFE—PRACTICAL APPLICATIONS AND STRATEGIES

When we hear stories like the ones above, we are apt to assume that negotiating the Broad Highway is always a grand odyssey. Like any good addict, we are probably attracted to the glamour of the spiritual path without fully realizing what we are getting into. But if we are fortunate, like Dennis, we may be able to get through our need to be special and find a way to keep it simple. Exploring the mystery of the Steps should ultimately *demystify* the riddles of everyday existence. It should bring us squarely back to ourselves, to our relationships and obligations, and to the tasks that are immediately in front of us day to day. We want to find a way to do what Angeles Arrien calls "walking the mystical path with practical feet." To that end, we will now provide some tips and clues that have been useful for many who have gone before us.

THE INNER HEALER AND MOVING TOWARD WHOLENESS

Many psychological and spiritual systems adhere to the belief that healing comes from within. They give this transformational power various interpretations, depending on whether they use a primarily mystical or psychological perspective. In some schools, it is called the "Higher Self," or the "soul." In others, it is simply referred to as a "healing mechanism." No matter what it is called, all systems are referring to that mysterious, and ultimately nameless, force within us that is in charge of our transformation. Many of us have come to call it the "inner healer."

Making the inner-healer concept an active part of daily practice has been an effective program tool for many seekers. According to Sri Aurobindo's philosophy, which we outlined in "The Stepdance," we and all of creation are involved in an eternal evolutionary process toward wholeness. And the dynamic that directs this evolution toward wholeness, or health, is the inner healer.

Whether we are focusing on it or not, we are always being guided from within toward health. If we can make this principle part of our new worldview, "our whole attitude and outlook upon life will change," as the Big Book promises. Instead of dreading the unknown parts of ourselves, we can begin to develop an abiding trust in the benign nature of transformation. We can make an article of faith out of our new belief that we are actually "doing it right." Thus at this far stage of our exploration do we come full circle to "Good News."

From this perspective, *everything we do, or go through, is ultimately an opportunity for healing*. In our daily life, we can employ the strategy we outlined in chapter 6, "The Treasure Trove," to approach a deep experiential session. At that time, we said that our responsibility was to "be with," or surrender as best we can, to whatever comes into our awareness, knowing that our inner healer is always moving us toward wholeness. In this identical fashion, we can address *every* issue that emerges into our consciousness at any part of the day or night.

We are being guided toward wholeness, whether we are in a therapy session or not. Remember, Aurobindo said that all life is a yoga. If we can somehow embrace *every* circumstance of our lives as an opportunity to improve our conscious contact, then we will discover that the Steps are truly a yoga. We will be working the Eleventh Step, and indeed *all* the Steps, in each moment.

Even what comes up for us in dreams can be understood as a way that our inner healer is moving us toward wholeness. In this case, we would use the same strategy as we do in our waking moments. We embrace the experience, allow whatever insight we may receive to emerge, and then practice a Sixth and Seventh Step. We become the witness, as well as the experiencer, of our own healing adventure.

Our lives take on the quality of a great experiment in transformation. In a sense, we are both the scientist and the subject of our own experiment. Somehow the Higher Power intimately involves us in the evolution of the universe itself. Our task is to open to and welcome the results of the universe experiment.

Ultimately, we learn that we are not *here* in order to get *somewhere else*. We give up trying to reach some far-off goal. What would we do if we got there? The adventure itself is the goal. Our purpose is to *be with what is*, as best we can. This means totally involving ourselves in a moment-to-moment process of surrender. When necessary, it means finding a safe setting in which to fully experience every deep emotion that emerges. It means welcoming and opening to the entire human and divine dance.

Sometimes, we may feel pushed beyond the comfort zone. Some teachers have said that the spiritual journey is like being a 110-volt circuit which is suddenly plugged in to a 220-volt outlet. It appears we are being asked to handle greater and greater dispensations of the energy of our Higher Power. This energy is a profound gift, but it can also be a frightening one. In a sense, we are being required to learn to live with a measure of "uncomfortability."

Our emotions may be more intense than we are accustomed to. As our bodies release the years of accumulated tension, we may feel overwhelmed for a while. But through this dramatic cycle, we can rely absolutely on the principles we know so well. We surrender to the discomfort as best we can. The more we can open and stretch our own limits, the easier it will be to allow the transformation to complete itself.

We discover that it is the place where we hold on that causes our tension. And where we hold on is like the ever-receding horizon line that we have mentioned so often. Each day we are confronted with a horizon line within ourselves. This horizon line has two sides. One side of the line is fear, the other surrender. In our own unique ways we must each face this place where we hold on and are afraid.

Each of these lines is a part of the archetypal struggle that all human beings must go through on the journey toward wholeness. And though the circumstances of our struggles are frequently different, the horizon line remains the same. Facing the fear at the horizon, and surrendering into a new place in consciousness, are how we reenact the universal process of death and rebirth every day. Life itself is an opportunity to make our First Step experience a daily practice of transformation. In this way, we become our yoga. We are the Tao, the Way. We awaken to our purpose of becoming as conscious as we can, allowing our Higher Power, as the inner healer, to be the guide. After all, as Ram Dass has said so beautifully, "What else is there to do?"

THE LINK BETWEEN DIMENSIONS

In our exploration, we have challenged the previously untouchable boundaries of birth and death. Our worldview has opened wide on the further dimensions of the psyche. Yet we are still apt to be perplexed as we consider the task of "bringing back home" the value of our experiences in these far-flung realms.

How can we distill the essence of these experiences into a practical, working life strategy? Is there some concept that can act as a bridge between our ordinary lives and our perinatal and transpersonal worlds?

Most of us are familiar with the term *pattern*, which we use to describe how a character defect plays itself out over a period of time in our lives. One way to visualize the nature of a pattern is to think of it as a string of beads. The thread on which the beads are strung is the central theme. Each bead is an experience that has the common theme as its core. The string of beads begins in this present moment and extends all the way back through our entire lifetime up to the time of our birth. However, we are now learning that the thread does not just stop there. It may actually recede through birth, into the perinatal dimension, and on into the collective realms of the psyche. In the collective dimension, the thread "unravels" and ceases to have a "linear" aspect. There the beads behave more like a constellation.

Probably the best way to explain how one of these patterns influences our lives and how we can work with them is to provide a real-life example of one. I have chosen to relate one of my own, because, for obvious reasons, I am quite familiar with it.

All through my childhood, adolescence, and young adulthood, I was a "stranger in a strange land." Somehow, I felt as though I had been washed up on the shores of earth. When I was little, I was so solemn that my parents used to call me Hamlet, Heathcliff, and the "Brooding Jeremiah."

Later, I found myself drawn to the great blues music of my native South. I also identified with certain songs by rock groups—"Gypsy," by the Moody Blues, "King of Pain," by the Police, "Alien," by the Atlanta Rhythm Section, and many more. I was attracted to anything that echoed the same sense of personal and cosmic aloneness that I had always felt. I never seemed to be able to have a successful relationship. Somehow, I always created situations where I would be alone, and then would feel victimized by my own orchestrations.

My early psychedelic experiences gave me my first sense of connectedness. But this was later overshadowed by the unbearable aloneness of my addiction. When I first entered the program,

I began to get some relief. Yet after I had been sober for a while, I realized that this aloneness was still very much a part of me. Even after doing some good family-of-origin and codependence work, the feeling was still there.

As I described in the introduction, in 1984 I began to use an Eleventh Step method to enrich my Twelve Step practice. After having had some beautiful spiritual experiences early on, I became aware of the most profound sense of aloneness I had ever known. It seemed to be the archetypal essence of every other experience of aloneness that I had ever had.

I realized that I had unwittingly touched a core level of my aloneness pattern that appeared to be the forerunner of all my biographical experiences of aloneness. During this phase of my exploration, I was also augmenting my inner work with outside study. It was then that I first learned that patterns can have roots in the birth process. For the first time, it was clear to me that I had uncovered what I could only call a birth pattern of aloneness. I now realized that there were other, deeper reasons why I had always felt alone. It was not just the result of what happened in my childhood, although that was certainly part of it. *I had been born with that feeling*.

At this point, my inner exploration took on the characteristics of an odyssey. Even though it was more painful than it had ever been before, I was able to trust that my inner healer would take me all the way through the pattern and out the other side. So I began to make friends with the "dark night of the soul."

Already, the healing had begun. For the first time, I was not just feeling *my* aloneness. I was experiencing the *archetype* of aloneness itself. I saw that the dark night of the soul was an experience common to all seekers. Knowing this, I realized that *I was not alone in my aloneness*. I was beginning to feel connected.

Later, I ran across some references to aloneness in some of the studies I was doing to help me integrate my inner experiences. I found a passage from the Sufi tradition that echoed my own sentiments. It read, "God, in the aloneness and solitude of his own unity." And in the great epic poem *Savitri*, by Sri Aurobindo, were the words, "God, the Ineffable, the Alone." At that point, I had what was for me a profound insight. In its aspect of oneness, before there is any creation of multiplicity, *the Higher Power too is alone*.

I felt that I had glimpsed the ultimate origin of aloneness. What's more, this aloneness was not something bad. It was, in fact, a noble quality that stemmed from the Higher Power itself, and as such was a positive attribute of all seekers who had ever traveled on the Broad Highway.

As I did more study, I came to realize that leaders in the field of psychology had been talking about patterns for quite some time and had already provided names for them. For example, Carl Jung referred to patterns as complexes. And more recently, Stanislav Grof called them COEX (pronounced "ko-ex") systems.

Before we demonstrate how to work with one of these strings of beads on a daily basis, we should first explain how something that has origins in the birth process can influence our lives. As we said before, we now understand that we are not a *tabula rasa*, or a clean slate, at the time of birth. We can think of the perinatal influence—in my case, the theme of "aloneness"—as somehow coloring or obscuring the lens through which we view our world. From the start, I saw every situation of my life through the lens of aloneness. Therefore, I tended to interpret every interaction I had with my environment as contributing to my isolation.

Because of the alcoholism in my family, there were obviously plenty of reasons why I could feel alone. However, there were many other situations which, in and of themselves, would not necessarily result in my reacting that way. Yet, because aloneness was already imprinted in my psyche, it tended to selectively reinforce my belief that I was alone. In this sense, a pattern has an energy that perpetuates itself and even contributes to shaping our reality.

One indication that we are participating in a pattern is that we will hear ourselves repeating, "I can't believe this is happening to me again." We usually make statements like this *before* we have begun the healing process. After we have done some work on the pattern, we find ourselves saying something like "I can't believe I'm still creating this situation in my life." One of the primary indications that we are healing is that we stop feeling victimized by our own actions and start taking responsibility for our part in creating the pattern. This echoes a profound passage in the Twelve and Twelve: "It is a spiritual axiom that every time we are disturbed, no matter what the cause, there is something wrong *with us*."

At this point we may wonder, Why do we repeat the pattern? How do we keep creating more beads on the string? The way we heal is that our Higher Power, through the inner healer, continually moves us toward wholeness by bringing unconscious material from our psyche into our awareness. Thus, in my case, I started life with an unconscious birth trauma characterized by aloneness. From the beginning, my inner healer continually attempted to make me aware of this pattern that needed to be healed. But for a long time I did not recognize the string. I only experienced the beads, or the *results* of my seeing the world with the eyes of aloneness.

Every time I felt victimized was an opportunity to make conscious what the inner healer was trying to show me. But the beads on my string of aloneness continued to add up. Finally, I got in touch with the perinatal core of the pattern. At that point, I saw how I had selectively viewed each situation in my life in terms of aloneness. And, more importantly, I understood how I had been an unwitting creator of my isolation. From the moment I became aware of how aloneness was operating in my life, I was in the transformational process.

Working with the entire string of beads eventually removes the color of the pattern from our viewing lens. We will know we have been healed of our patterns when we can see our objective existence *for what it is*, instead of acting as though it were our *personal play*. As long as we experience life colored by unconscious influences, we are essentially in denial of the inherent clarity and fullness of human existence. We cannot truly "be with what is" until "what is" is more than just our reactions to forces of which we are unaware.

Making conscious the fact that we are caught in a pattern initiates healing, but it does not necessarily complete it. It does not mean that we will not add a few more beads to the string. It just means that we will not unconsciously repeat the pattern as often and feel as victimized by it as we did in the past. The key to our continued work with a newly recognized thread is *consciousness* itself. Here is a metaphor that may help explain how we can work with a pattern in our daily lives.

We may think of the string of beads as being a steam-powered locomotive roaring down the track at about eighty miles an hour. We can also envision ourselves as being the one who is responsible for stoking the fire with coal. The reason the train is going so fast is that we have been stoking the fire for a long time—at least for our whole lives, our birth, and possibly even longer than that. Our problem is that we now want the train to stop.

At first, we expect somebody else to make it stop. But meanwhile we go right on stoking. And when it does not come to a halt, we feel that somebody else must be responsible and is somehow doing this to us. Then we receive the startling insight that *we* are the reason the train is going so fast. All we have to do is *stop feeding the fire*. So we put down the shovel and sit back. But again, *nothing happens*. The train is *still* hurtling down the track at somewhere close to eighty miles an hour.

Our patterns are not going to disappear simply because we discover that we *have* them, any more than the locomotive will come to an abrupt halt just because we stop stoking the fire. This train weighs many tons and has a roaring fire going under the boiler. And, what's more important, it has *momentum*. This momentum would carry it a long way down the track, *even if we did not stoke the fire anymore*. But the problem is, we frequently *forget* that we are the ones feeding coal into the fire. We go *unconscious* again. The next thing we know is that we "come to," somewhere way down the track, and find that we have again been stoking the fire.

This time, however, we stay conscious longer, sit back again, and *witness* how the train is gradually slowing down. We do not know how long it will take for the accumulated power of the fire we have already built to burn itself out. *Every pattern has momentum*. Our responsibility during this time is to be as conscious as we can while the train is slowing down, and to reawaken as soon as possible after those inevitable times when we find ourselves stoking the fire again.

This is the way patterns play themselves out in our daily lives. They will not cease to affect us just because we make them conscious. However, we *will* discover that we will not be a *victim* of them as much as we were in the past. And we will be less hampered by them as we pursue the fulfillment of our everyday relationships. Gradually, we experience them almost as "old friends" instead of enemies who have the potential to ruin our lives. We are not certain that we will ever be entirely free of our patterns. But we are sure that it is possible to live with them as though they were just a few more interesting twists of plot in our universe play.

CONCLUSION—KEEPING IT SIMPLE

By the time recovery found me, I had already been graced with many experiences in other dimensions of the psyche. As I said in the introduction, I knew how to fly. My problem was living on planet Earth. If at that time I had climbed the Himalayas to the cave of a holy woman, she would have told me to stay clean, get a toothbrush, support my family, and be at work on time. *The most spiritual thing I could do was to take care of each part of my human existence that was directly in front of me*. And this is even more true today.

The Buddhist teacher Jack Kornfield says that if we want to find out how spiritual we are, we should ask our spouses. If spiritual exploration is worth anything at all, we must be able to apply our realizations to everyday reality, especially with the ones who are closest to us. When we look at the adventure from this perspective, it does not take us long to feel humbled by just how far we still have to go.

The spiritual life seems to be about becoming fully human. And even though we have found that humanness is much richer than we ever realized, this in no way diminishes the importance of living our lives as individuals in relationship with other individuals. In fact, our new insights should serve to enhance the sacredness and the beauty of what we have previously referred to as the "ordinary life."

Our ultimate response to receiving the ever-expanding riches of the Twelve Steps can only be a profound sense of gratitude. Compared to what we have been given, what we can actually give in return seems to be quite little. Making our lives a moment-to-moment expression of this gratitude appears to be the only way to communicate what we truly feel about the miracle of recovery. We have been blessed, and we continue to be blessed, each moment that we open anew to the mystery of the Steps.

CHAPTER ELEVEN

The Big Twelfth Step—Recovery and the Planet

If humanity is to survive, a radical transformation of human nature is indispensible.

—Sri Aurobindo

Though we in A.A. find ourselves living in a world characterized by destructive fears as never before in history, we see great areas of faith, and tremendous aspirations toward justice and brotherhood. Yet no prophet can assume to say whether the world outcome will be blazing destruction or the beginning, under God's intention, of the brightest era yet known to mankind.

—Bill W.

Our Twelve Steps, when simmered down to the last, resolve themselves into the words "love" and "service."

—Dr. Bob

Addiction is the ultimate condition of separation. And any comprehensive philosophy of recovery must include the experience of wholeness. But wholeness is not a one-shot deal. If we have learned anything from our adventure into the mystery of the Steps, it is that recovery is a horizon which ever recedes the more we travel toward it. We have also seen how the individual journey from separation toward wholeness is a microcosm of the evolution of all creation toward a similar state of oneness. None of us really knows what the ultimate experience of wholeness will be. In addition, we are apt to wonder if it might not somehow entail the loss of our individuality and uniqueness altogether.

Over and over, we have seen how truth is often a paradox. Two seemingly contradictory concepts *can* coexist in the same philosophy. We have begun to accept the fact of contradiction and to see it not as an "either/or proposition," but as a "both/and." This is the principle of complementarity we have used throughout the text. And now, once again, complementarity reveals itself to be a key element in this current recovery phase. Moving toward wholeness and oneness does not negate our individuality, but in fact enhances our uniqueness. *Both individuality and oneness* are vital components of a Twelve Step yoga.

Thus far, we have explored the mysteries of the Steps as they reveal themselves to individuals on the Broad Highway. Now it is time to envision what effect many thousands of individuals moving toward wholeness may have on humanity and on the planet itself. Judging from the current crises of planetary evolution, our discussion seems quite timely.

THE FIRST ADDICTIONS THERAPIST

The most profound and all-encompassing metaphor for addiction and recovery is so old that it is almost new. This universal definition is to be found in Buddha's Four Noble Truths. The First Truth states that life contains suffering. The Second explains that suffering is caused by craving, attachment, and unfulfilled desire. As we said previously, our modern word for this craving, or attachment, is *addiction*. The Third Truth lets us know that there is a way out of suffering. And the Fourth demonstrates what the way out is by outlining the Eightfold Way.

The Four Truths directly relate to the Twelve Steps. Accepting the truth of suffering, and that suffering is caused by addiction, is the action of the First Step. That there is a way out falls under the domain of the Second. And the Fourth Truth, or the Eightfold Way, corresponds to the rest of the Steps and "how recovery works."

The Buddha's description of the basic problem of human suffering as attachment demonstrates that addiction is a universal human dilemma. The fact that the Steps are devoted to the alleviation of this condition, in the same fashion that the Buddha prescribed the practice of the Eightfold Way, elevates the Steps once more to the ranks of the great traditions of the world. As the recovery metaphor evolves, we can look to the future for new definitions. But ironically, one of the newest requires us to look back into the distant past. There we discover that one of the greatest thinkers of our planet, the Buddha, was also the first true recovery pioneer.

PLAYING WITH METAPHORS

A metaphor is a way of talking about truth. It is not *the* truth. A metaphor is a story that acts as a vehicle to convey certain themes and nuances of a larger, and ultimately unexplainable, reality. Becoming able to view life in terms of metaphor demonstrates that we are being freed from our addiction to thinking we know "how it all is." Recovery lets us "wear the world like a loose garment" and not get caught in any one limited perspective of reality. As we move toward wholeness, we can more readily see how *all* metaphors contain truth and how each is part of the whole picture.

What we are basically describing is an expansion of consciousness beyond our merely personal worldviews. To assist ourselves in this expansion, we can become the recipients of the gifts of the ages in the form of metaphors that describe evolution toward wholeness. These gifts come from all eras. We have characterized recovery as the "Tao," or the Way. Joseph Campbell gives us the story of the "Hero's Journey." Stan Grof calls exploration the "Adventure of Self-Discovery." And the Big Book describes the road to recovery as the "Broad Highway."

Linking these metaphors synthesizes the recovery story with psychology, spirituality, and the dimensions of mythology and archetype. Experiencing our journey as one of these stories, or as one of the many we have not mentioned, takes us out of the narrow confines of ourselves. Our search is elevated to the ranks of world odysseys. The value of this amplification, in terms of recovery, is that we are gradually freed from our egos. We then experience ourselves not just as one with other addicts, but as one with humanity itself.

ADDICTION AND THE PLANET

In 1992, at a conference in Prague, Czechoslovakia, on bringing together science and spirituality, there was a prominent addiction and recovery track. That addiction and recovery were highlighted at this gathering of world teachers and seekers demonstrates the recognition by the world community of the profound importance of these conditions to global transformation.

The transpersonal perspective reveals that this crisis extends far beyond the problems we normally recognize as addictions. As we hope we have demonstrated, addiction is basic to the fabric of the human condition. Alcoholism, as well as drug, food, work, sex, and gambling addiction, is symptomatic of a much more pervasive dilemma that is actually threatening survival of life on the planet. In one sense, this deeper malaise can be seen as an addiction to power and control.

This perverse tendency relies on the philosophy that "more is better," and fosters the relentless pursuit of unlimited linear growth. On a global scale, this trajectory may ultimately end in wholesale ecological pollution, which could render our planet uninhabitable. We blindly turn our backs on humanitarian responsibilities in our own backyard. And we sit by while the rest of the world takes on the struggle of protecting the global environment. The collapse of Communism notwithstanding, the continued violation of human rights and the gross inequities between the wealthy and the destitute demonstrate the insidious nature of power addiction worldwide.

In his address at the conference in Prague, Ram Dass hinted that the United States, and the Western tradition altogether, may soon go through a death. This process appears to have already begun. Just as individual addicts in denial struggle to maintain their addictions, our culture is fighting for its survival. We are a society in denial of that which could destroy us. And what might destroy us is not some evil "out there," but in fact exists within us, as our collective ego.

It is arrogance to assume that because we think we have "won" a victory over Communism, we will not have to undergo profound changes ourselves. But at the current moment, it seems almost impossible for us to own our insatiable addiction to power and greed. How long we can continue on this "linear binge" we can only guess. But it is inevitable that the timeless cycle of death and rebirth will reclaim our society, as it has reclaimed us in our individual recovery. Although it may be painful, as in fact it already is, we as a culture must experience our powerlessness. We must surrender to the evolution of world culture toward a wholeness that can only truly be envisioned in the mind of the Higher Power.

THE ARCHETYPES OF ADDICTION AND RECOVERY

The addiction crisis of the twentieth century is a microcosm of the universal human dilemma. The way we have been forced to address the problems of alcoholism and other forms of addiction represents a powerful spotlight thrown directly on this archetypal human condition. Addiction is the most obvious and articulate way that modern humanity could make conscious the universal problem of attachment. Addiction is first and foremost a spiritual dilemma.

We can think of the modern addiction crisis as the way the timeless archetype of Attachment has manifested itself in our time. But just as every crisis has a way out, the addiction problem also has a solution. This is the archetype of Recovery. The archetype of Recovery is one of the principal ways that the Higher Power has introduced universal spiritual principles into the lives of modern seekers. The solution to the addiction crisis is spirituality. The solution to the planetary crisis is exactly the same.

Just as individuals experience the death of addiction into the rebirth of recovery, world society is also undergoing the death/rebirth process of moving toward wholeness. That the addiction crisis and the spiritual solution have occurred in the twentieth century is a sign of the imminent necessity of global awakening.

Without this global awakening, which is the result of millions of individuals undergoing death and rebirth in their own lives, it seems less likely that we can survive. Yet there is hope. Changes have already begun. Side by side with the crises we have mentioned are tremendous advances in spiritual growth by people all over the world. More than ever, we are becoming a world family. And just as it is always darkest before the dawn, we are possibly on the brink of a greater collective rebirth than we have yet experienced.

Modern society's most pervasive condition, addiction, will lead us to embrace the great spiritual traditions of the past in a way that is modernized and made relevant for us in today's world. It will become the gateway to planetary healing. We have experienced the individual awakening. Now we can look forward to the renaissance of the human family at large.

HERESIES

As we near the end of our exploration, it would not hurt to stretch our limits perhaps one more time. Now that we have become accustomed to "new ideas," let's explore a few that may challenge some of the beliefs we have previously held sacred. Because these may rattle our cage just a little bit, we will refer to them as "heresies."

The principle of complementarity teaches us that we should honor both our separateness and our connections with each other. Even though 1935 was the birth date of AA, it also marked the beginning of the *Twelve Step movement. Both* these events are important. The Twelve Steps are the core creative force behind recovery. Their power lies at the heart of all fellowships. This is why we can speak of a Twelve Step movement that is larger, and in some ways more important, than AA or any other single "anonymous."

In a sense, the Twelve Step movement represents the archetype of the recovery community of which all fellowships are a part. If we cannot honor this sense of unity *at the same time* that we celebrate our uniqueness, it is possible that we will be left behind by a humanity that is more and more recognizing its oneness. We cut ourselves off from the life-giving force of the Higher Power by championing exclusivity at the expense of comprehensiveness. After all, our purpose is to carry the message to others.

What kind of people will these "others" be in the years to come? First of all, we would hope that more and more young seekers will be led to enter a fellowship. But speaking as a father, I can say that my children are much more sophisticated than I was at their age. This is in part the result of the natural evolution of humanity toward wholeness. But for whatever reason, we must be able to stretch our metaphorical boundaries to include the language and worldview of these future generations. If we cannot, then we miss the opportunity to be of service to our young ones. We cannot just expect them to relate to us. *We must open ourselves to relate to them.*

Another group coming into fellowships more frequently is made up of those who have already been on the spiritual journey and who are just beginning to discover the power of addiction in their own lives. These seekers have perhaps come a long way already on the Broad Highway and may be quite psychologically sophisticated. We must be able to meet this group where they are on the road and help them feel that recovery can benefit them as well.

The flowering of the feminist perspective also forces us to reexamine some of the basic metaphors we have all used to explain recovery. Unfortunately, there is probably no way around the fact that AA was founded by two men at a time when addiction was seen as a condition that primarily affected men. Nor can we escape the inherently masculine metaphor of the Big Book itself. But if this is the case, what are the implications for women? It is the height of arrogance to expect women just to "live with it." Yet this dilemma does seem to be another catch-22.

Already there are a number of good recovery books that focus specifically on the needs of seekers who are women. These even include some that have undertaken the adventure of rewording the Steps to give them more of a feminine perspective. Before we lash out at this "heresy," we must consider the ultimate goal of the recovery journey. We are moving away from exclusivity and toward inclusiveness. In that spirit, let us welcome all creative innovations that make recovery more accessible to seekers everywhere.

In this text, we have already explored a deep recovery concept that can serve to alter the perception of the fellowships as "patriarchy." I believe that understanding the Twelve Steps as a death/rebirth mystery school demonstrates that the recovery process is ultimately deeply rooted in the Divine Feminine. Death and rebirth, and the cycles of fertility and nature, are all feminine principles. Surrender too is a feminine dynamic. In this sense, recovery itself seems to be a feminine response to an inherently egoic, or masculine, condition.

We hope these deeper understandings of the mysteries of recovery will help seekers "re-vision" traditional recovery metaphors and to open the doors on a new feminist perspective of the Twelve Steps. We must be willing to let go of the "letter" of recovery to make room for the "spirit" of transformation. Remember, only the power of the Twelve Steps is unchanging. But *how* we understand the Steps will always evolve.

The evolution of recovery science over the past half century has been marked with many breakthroughs that are no less than quantum leaps. The Twelve Steps, and the fundamental principle of abstinence, may be the only things that have not changed at least somewhat. Nothing else is etched in stone. Who knows what recovery will look like at the turn of the century?

The metaphor of codependence has dominated the eighties and early nineties. We owe much of its basic philosophy to the humanistic era of psychology. And we are just now realizing how much codependence also has in common with the universal dilemma described by Buddha in his Four Noble Truths. Suffering is caused by unfulfilled desire. Or, as the codependence field suggests, it is caused by seeking fulfillment in areas that are inherently unable to provide that fulfillment.

We as individual seekers let go of outdated personal stories in favor of newer ones that more accurately depict our current stage of growth. In the same way, collective recovery metaphors will inevitably outlive their usefulness. We must be willing to let go of old recovery stories, if doing so will mean the influx of a fresh dispensation of creative energy from the Higher Power. Even though the *essence* of the codependence metaphor and other elements of recovery philosophy will remain, the *form* may change.

Already some of the best-known figures in the recovery movement, such as John Bradshaw, Rokelle Lerner, Jane Middelton-Moz, Charles Whitfield, and Anne Wilson Schaef are looking ahead to new spiritual perspectives. And transpersonal teachers, such as Christina Grof, the author of *The Thirst for Wholeness*, are forging new syntheses that re-vision the recovery journey.

Whenever we think *This is the way it is*, we are placing an arbitrary limit on the possibilities of transformation. No sooner do we establish ourselves on the beachhead of some idea about reality than the waves of change come to wash our ideas away. We might become, as the old program saying says, "bleeding deacons," hanging on to the way it used to be. Each time we draw the line and claim to have found the answer, we must prepare ourselves for the adventure of death and rebirth.

It seems we will be required to surrender all that we are and everything we think to our Higher Power. A Zen abbot once said that any small story is an ugly one. The most beautiful story is the whole one—the *big picture*. Since none of us can claim to have the big picture, our best bet is to practice living in the "*don't know*" place. After all, in the face of the mystery, how can we actually claim to really *know* anything? One of the best yogas for us seems to be the moment-to-moment process of surrendering to the mystery—and not having to know.

CONCLUSION—ON THE BROAD HIGHWAY

My first sponsor, who is dead now, was one of the most naturally spiritual persons I have ever known. He never heard of archetypes or consciousness research. Yet he was the archetype of Humility. After I had attended my first experiential Eleventh Step intensive, I wanted to share my experience with him. But I was afraid to, because I did not think he would understand. After I told him what had happened, he said, "That's great, sounds like you had a spiritual experience *on your retreat*."

He *knew*. It was nothing fancy to him. He was a living embodiment of the principles of the Twelve Steps. He was the finest Twelve Step seeker I have ever known. I tell this story here to point out that the journey of this text is just *one way* to describe the recovery adventure. There are as many different Twelve Step yogas as there are seekers working the Steps. If we use Sri Aurobindo's definition, there are as many yogas as there are people on the planet. For, as he said, all life is a yoga. It is definitely not necessary to envision the Twelve Step adventure in the way that we do here. But it is important that we open to the way our Higher Power will unfold it uniquely for each of us.

We can appreciate what the recovery pioneers must have felt when they began to "make a case for spirituality." They must have asked themselves how they were going to be able to introduce the fact of spirituality to a public that would probably resist such ideas. But they succeeded. The Big Book does a masterful job of presenting these revolutionary principles.

There will never be another Big Book. But we are told that more will be disclosed. If this is true, then where will it be disclosed? Each of us is required to be our own "big book." The evolution of recovery truth will unfold in the lives of each of us. And it seems that we may face some of the same difficulties that the founding members had when they first introduced the spiritual perspective. I hope this text makes a case for its own unique allotment of experience, strength, and hope.

Each of us probably has our own special passages from the Big Book we are fond of quoting. For me, there are two. The first of these is, "Our real purpose is to fit ourselves to be of maximum service to God and the people about us." This passage does not just say "service," or "a little service." It says *maximum* service. "Maximum" is a lot of service! It implies that we must serve to the utmost of our abilities. Only a lifetime spent in making a yoga out of service would fulfill the aim of this statement.

Moreover, the passage says "our *real* purpose." Our task cannot be spelled out much more clearly than that. However, after traveling some distance beyond the crossroads, we are amazed to discover that the "people about us" include many more than we ever dreamed. In fact, we ultimately realize that this phrase refers to the entire human family. Our work begins within. But our new understanding of the Twelve Step mysteries shows us how we are one with humanity. What we do individually affects the whole. This is why we are asked to serve the people about us to the maximum extent that we are able.

The second sentence has been quoted frequently already. It says, "We are sure our Higher Power means for us to be happy, joyous, and free." These three gifts stretch before us on the ever-receding horizon we have mentioned so often. We do not know their limits. But we can add to our worldview that wonderful concept of *ananda*. If we choose, we can believe, just as the ancients did, that the very fabric of existence itself is joy. From this perspective, we can foresee that one of the purposes of our journey is to *become* the happiness, joy, and freedom that is at the heart of all creation.

Bill W. called this truth the "Great Fact." He says that we will get the answers we need if "our house is in order." And what a house it is! It certainly is not what we thought it was before we began our adventure. This house turns out to be no less than the whole universe. We are told to abandon ourselves. To actually conceive of letting go that completely takes us into the archetype of Surrender itself. Yet this seems to be what the Twelve Steps have been pointing to all along.

In the final sentence of "A Vision for You" in the Big Book, Bill W. talks about "trudging" the "Road of Happy Destiny." We are beginning to know this road. We came to it at a crossing a while ago. We then made the decision to follow our Higher Power through the crossroads and on into the mysteries of the Steps. The Road of Happy Destiny and the Broad Highway are one and the same. We find ourselves journeying in the company of seekers from all paths everywhere and for all time. As the text says, we may have "trudged" at some point in our adventure. But we might not be surprised to soon find ourselves *dancing* down the road we were once afraid even to walk upon.

We are answering the call, even though we are uncertain where the call will lead us. The horizons of spirituality will always be a mystery. But we *are* witnessing recovery taking its place alongside the world's great spiritual movements. We sense as well that the call is currently signaling a global shift toward wholeness. We find ourselves hoping that spirituality in *all* its forms can be the key to planetary survival. And we are excited and humbled to be a part of this adventure.

We are moving into a "wholeness paradigm" of recovery. The Higher Power will inevitably lead us down the Broad Highway toward this wholeness. We must open to wholeness and embrace it as fully as we can. How do we do this? For Twelve Step practice, it means taking the Eleventh Step—and *all* the Steps—literally, as the founding members of the movement meant for them to be taken. It means a no-holds-barred opening to the possibilities of the radical awakening.

The Twelve Steps are the greatest contribution to perennial philosophy of our age. It is with a great sense of gratitude that we are finally beginning to recognize a small part of the gift that has been given us. And finally, it seems fitting to close with the words of Bill W., from July 1960: "Our high aim can be emotional sobriety, full emotional maturity—and that's good. However, I think most of us may prefer a still larger definition, one with a still broader and higher reach. Perhaps there can be no 'relative' in the universe unless somewhere there is an 'absolute.' To most of us this 'absolute' is 'God as we understand Him.' We feel that we were born to this life to grow—if only a little—toward that likeness and image."

So, leave it to the Higher Power. . . .

—Ramana Maharshi

THE TWELVE STEPS OF ALCOHOLICS ANONYMOUS*

1. We admitted we were powerless over alcohol—that our lives had become unmanageable.
2. Came to believe that a Power greater than ourselves could restore us to sanity.
3. Made a decision to turn our will and our lives over to the care of God *as we understood Him*.
4. Made a searching and fearless moral inventory of ourselves.
5. Admitted to God, to ourselves, and to another human being the exact nature of our wrongs.
6. Were entirely ready to have God remove all these defects of character.
7. Humbly asked Him to remove our shortcomings.
8. Made a list of all persons we had harmed, and became willing to make amends to them all.
9. Made direct amends to such people wherever possible, except when to do so would injure them or others.
10. Continued to take personal inventory and when we were wrong promptly admitted it.
11. Sought through prayer and meditation to improve our conscious contact with God *as we understood Him*, praying only for knowledge of His will for us and the power to carry that out.
12. Having had a spiritual awakening as the result of these steps, we tried to carry this message to alcoholics, and to practice these principles in all our affairs.

---

*The Twelve Steps of A.A. are taken from *Alcoholics Anonymous*, 3rd ed., published by A.A. World Services, Inc., New York, N.Y., 59-60. Reprinted with permission of A.A. World Services, Inc. (See editor's note on the copyright page.)

Bibliography

Alcoholics Anonymous World Services, Inc. *Alcoholics Anonymous*. New York: A.A. World Services, Inc., 1976.

———. *As Bill Sees It*. New York: A.A. World Services, Inc., 1967.

———. *The Language of the Heart*. New York: A.A. Grapevine, Inc., 1988.

———. *Pass It On*. New York: A.A. World Services, Inc., 1984.

———. *Twelve Steps and Twelve Traditions*. New York: A.A. World Services, Inc., 1981.

Arieti, Silvano. *Creativity: The Magic Synthesis*. New York: Basic Books, Inc., 1980.

Arrien, Angeles. *The Four-Fold Way*. San Francisco: Harper San Francisco, 1992.

———. *Signs of Life*. Sonoma, Calif.: Arcus, 1992.

Assagioli, Roberto. *Psychosynthesis*. New York: Penguin Books, 1971.

*Aurobindo, Sri. *Essays on the Gita*. Pondicherry, India: Sri Aurobindo Ashram, 1922.

———. *The Future Poetry*. Pondicherry, India: Sri Aurobindo Ashram, 1953.

———. *Savitri: A Legend and a Symbol*. Pondicherry, India: Sri Aurobindo Ashram, 1951.

———. *The Secret of the Veda*. Pondicherry, India: Sri Aurobindo Ashram, 1956.

———. *The Synthesis of Yoga*. Pondicherry, India: Sri Aurobindo Ashram, 1955.

———. *The Upanishads*. Pondicherry, India: Sri Aurobindo Ashram, 1971.

---

*Sri Aurobindo's books are available through Auromere, Inc., Pomona, California, 1-800-735-4691.

Bateson, Gregory. *Steps to an Ecology of Mind*. San Francisco: Chandler, 1972.

Beck, Charlotte Joko *Everyday Zen*. San Francisco: Harper San Francisco, 1989.

Blum, Ralph. *The Book of Runes: A Handbook for the Use of an Ancient and Contemporary Oracle*. New York: St. Martin's Press, 1982.

Bly, Robert. *Iron John*. New York: Addison-Wesley, 1990.

Bolen, Jean S. *Goddesses in Everywoman: A New Psychology of Women*. San Francisco: HarperCollins, 1985.

———. *Gods in Everyman: A New Psychology of Men's Lives and Loves*. San Francisco: Harper San Francisco, 1989.

Bopp, Judie, et al. *The Sacred Tree*. Wilmot, Wis.: Lotus Light, 1990.

Brown, Molly Young. *The Unfolding Self*. Los Angeles: Psychosynthesis Press, 1983.

Browne, Ivor. "Psychological Trauma, or Unexperienced Experience." *ReVision* 12 (1987). Washington, D.C.: Heldref Publications.

Campbell, Joseph. *The Hero with a Thousand Faces*. Princeton: Princeton University Press, 1990.

———. *Myths to Live By*. New York: Bantam, 1972.

Capra, Fritjof. *The Tao of Physics: An Exploration of the Parallels Between Modern Physics and Eastern Mysticism*. Boston: Shambhala Publications, 1975.

Dalai Lama. *A Human Approach to World Peace*. London: Wisdom Publications, 1984.

Dawes, Nigel. *Massage Cures: The Family Guide to Curing Common Ailments with Simple Massage Techniques*. London: HarperCollins, 1990.

Deikman, Arthur J. *The Observing Self: Mysticism and Psychotherapy*. Boston: Beacon Press, 1982.

Feild, Reshad. *Steps to Freedom: Discourses on the Alchemy of the Heart*. Brattleboro, Vt.: Threshold Books, 1983.

Ferrucci, Piero. *What We May Be: Techniques for Psychological and Spiritual Growth Through Psychosynthesis*. Los Angeles: Jeremy Tarcher, Inc., 1982

Feuerstein, Georg. *The Yoga-Sutras of Patanjali*. Rochester, Vt.: Inner Traditions, 1990.

———. *Yoga: The Technology of Ecstasy*. Los Angeles: Jeremy Tarcher, Inc., 1989

Fields, Rick, et al. *Chop Wood, Carry Water: A Guide to Finding Spiritual Fulfillment in Everyday Life*. Los Angeles: Jeremy Tarcher, Inc., 1984

Foundation for Inner Peace. *A Course in Miracles*. Glen Ellen, Calif.: Foundation for Inner Peace, 1975.

Fox, Matthew. *The Coming of the Cosmic Christ*. New York: Harper and Row, 1988.

———. *Original Blessing*. Santa Fe: Bear and Co., 1983.

Goldstein, Joseph, and Jack Kornfield. *Seeking the Heart of Wisdom: The Path of Insight Meditation*. Boston: Shambhala, 1987.

Grof, Christina. *The Thirst for Wholeness*. San Francisco: Harper San Francisco, 1993.

Grof, Christina, and Stanislav Grof. *The Stormy Search for Self*, Los Angeles: Jeremy Tarcher, Inc., 1990.

Grof, Stanislav. *The Adventure of Self-Discovery*. Albany: State University of New York Press, 1988.

———. *Beyond the Brain: Birth, Death, and Transcendence in Psychotherapy*. Albany: State University of New York Press, 1985.

———. *Human Survival and Consciousness Evolution*. Albany: State University of New York Press, 1988.

Grof, Stanislav, with Bennett, Hal Z. *The Holotropic Mind: The Three Levels of Human Consciousness and How They Shape Our Lives*. San Francisco: HarperCollins, 1992.

Grof, Stanislav, and Christina Grof. *Beyond Death: The Gates of Consciousness*. Albany: State University of New York Press, 1980.

Grof, Stanislav, ed. *Ancient Wisdom and Modern Science*. Albany: State University of New York Press, 1984.

Grof, Stanislav, and Christina Grof., eds. *Spritual Emergency*. Albany: State University of New York Press, 1989.

Hall, Calvin S., and Vernon J. Nordby. *A Primer of Jungian Psychology*. New York: The New American Library, 1973.

Hanh, Thich N. *Peace Is Every Step*. New York: Bantam, 1991.

Hardy, Jean. *Psychology with a Soul*. New York: Viking, 1988.

Harner, Michael. *The Way of the Shaman*. New York Bantam, 1982.

Hesse, Hermann. *Siddhartha*. New York: Bantam, 1982.

Huang, Chungliang Al. *Embrace Tiger, Return to Mountain: The Essence of Tai Ji*. Berkeley: Celestial Arts, 1988.

Huxley, Aldous. *The Doors of Perception*. New York: Harper and Row, 1954.

James, William. *The Varieties of Religious Experience*. New York: The New American Library, 1958.

Jellinek, E. M. *The Disease Concept of Alcoholism.* New Haven: Hillhouse Press, 1960.
Johnson, Vernon. *I'll Quit Tomorrow.* San Francisco: Harper and Row, 1980.
Jung, Carl G. *Man and His Symbols.* New York: Doubleday, 1972.
———. *Memories, Dreams, Reflections.* New York: Pantheon, 1961.
Kavanaugh, Kieran, and Otilio Rodriguez, trans. *The Collected Works of St. John of the Cross.* Washington, D.C.: ICS Publications, 1979.
Keen, Sam. *Fire in the Belly: On Being a Man.* New York: Bantam, 1991.
Khan, Pir Vilayat I. *Introducing Spirituality Into Counseling and Therapy.* New Lebanon, N.Y.: Omega Publications New York, 1982.
———. *Toward the One.* New York: Harper Colophon Books, 1974.
Kornfield, Jack, and Paul Breiter. *A Still Forest Pool.* Wheaton, Ill.: The Theosophical Publishing House, 1985.
Lao Tsu. *Tao Te Ching.* Ed. Gia-Fu Feng. Trans. Jane English. New York: Random House, 1972.
Larsen, Earnie. *Stage Two Recovery.* Minneapolis: Winston Press, Inc., 1985.
Lee, John. *The Flying Boy: Healing the Wounded Man.* Austin, Tex.: New Men's Press, 1987.
———. *I Don't Want to Be Alone.* Deerfield Beach, Fla.: Health Communications, 1990.
LeShan, Lawrence. *How to Meditate: A Guide to Self-Discovery.* New York: Bantam, 1984.
Leonard, Linda. *On the Way to the Wedding: Transforming the Love Relationship.* Boston: Shambhala, 1987.
———. *Witness to the Fire: Creativity and the Veil of Addiction.* Boston: Shambhala, 1989.
———. *The Wounded Woman: Healing the Father-Daughter Relationship.* Athens, Ohio: Ohio University Press, 1982.
Levine, Stephen. *A Gradual Awakening.* New York: Doubleday, Anchor Press, 1979.
———. *Who Dies: An Investigation of Conscious Living and Dying.* Garden City: Doubleday, Anchor Books, 1982.
Lidell, Lucy. *The Book of Massage.* New York: Simon and Schuster, 1984.
Maslow, Abraham. *Religions, Values and Peak-Experiences.* Columbus: Ohio State University Press, 1964.

———. *Toward a Psychology of Being*. Princeton: Van Nostrand, 1962.

May, Gerald. *Addiction and Grace*. New York: Harper and Row, 1982.

McNiff, Shaun. *The Arts and Psychotherapy*. Springfield, Ill.: Charles C. Thomas, 1981.

Moore, Robert, and Douglas Gillette. *King, Warrior, Magician, Lover: Rediscovering the Archetypes of the Mature Masculine*. San Francisco: Harper San Francisco, 1990.

Muktananda, Swami. *Play of Consciousness*. New York: Harper and Row, 1974.

N.A. World Service Office, Inc. *Narcotics Anonymous*. Van Nuys: N.A. World Service Office, Inc., 1984.

Neihardt, John G. *Black Elk Speaks*. New York: Pocket Books, 1932.

Ram Dass. *Be Here Now, Remember*. New York: Crown Publishing, 1971.

———. *The Journey of Awakening: A Mediator's Guidebook*. New York: Bantam, 1978.

———. *The Only Dance There Is*. Garden City: Anchor Books, 1974.

Ram Dass and Paul Gorman. *How Can I Help? Stories and Reflections on Service*. New York: Alfred A. Knopf, 1985.

Ram Dass and Stephen Levine. *Grist for the Mill*. Berkeley: Celestial Arts, 1987.

Ring, Kenneth. *Heading Toward Omega: In Search of the Meaning of the Near-Death Experience*. New York: Morrow, 1985.

Roth, Gabrielle. *Maps to Ecstasy: Teachings of an Urban Shaman*. London: New World Library, 1989.

Singer, June. *Boundaries of the Soul*. Garden City: Doubleday, Anchor Books, 1972.

Sparks, Tav. "To Hell and Back—One Addict's Journey." In *To Be a Man*, ed. Keith Thompson. Los Angeles: Jeremy Tarcher, Inc., 1991.

———. "Transpersonal Treatment of Addictions—Radical Return to Roots." *ReVision* 10 (1987): Washington, D.C.: Heldref Publications.

Starhawk. *The Spiral Dance*. New York: Harper and Row, 1979.

Steindl-Rast, David. *Gratefulness, The Heart of Prayer: An Approach to Life in Fullness*. New York: Paulist Press, 1984.

———. *A Listening Heart*. New York: Crossroads, 1983.

Suzuki, Shunryu. *Zen Mind, Beginner's Mind*. New York: John Weatherhill, 1970.

Tarnas, Richard. *The Passion of the Western Mind: Understanding the Ideas That Have Shaped Our World View*. New York: Harmony Books, 1991.

Thompson, Keith, ed. *To Be a Man*. Los Angeles: Jeremy Tarcher, Inc., 1991.

Tiebout, Harry M. *The Tiebout Papers*. Center City, Minn.: Hazelden Educational Materials, 1972.

Trungpa, Chogyam. *Cutting Through Spiritual Materialism*. Boston: Shambhala, 1973.

Vaughan, Frances E. *Awakening Intuition*. New York: Doubleday, 1979.

Vaughan, Frances, and Roger Walsh, eds. *Accept This Gift*. Los Angeles: Jeremy Tarcher, Inc., 1983

Walsh, Roger. *The Spirit of Shamanism*. Los Angeles: Jeremy Tarcher, Inc., 1990.

Walsh, Roger, and Frances Vaughan, eds. *Beyond Ego: Transpersonal Dimensions in Psychology*. Los Angeles: Jeremy Tarcher, Inc., 1980.

Waters, Frank. *Book of the Hopi*. New York: Ballantine, 1963.

Watts, Alan. *This Is It*. New York: Random, 1973.

Wegscheider-Cruse, Sharon. *Another Chance*. Palo Alto: Science and Behavior Books, 1981.

Whitfield, Charles. *Co-Dependence: Healing the Human Condition*. Deerfield Beach, Fla.: Health Communications, 1991.

———. *Healing the Child Within*. Deerfield Beach, Fla.: Health Communications, 1987.

Wilber, Ken. *The Atman Project*. Wheaton, Ill.: The Theosophical Publishing House, 1980.

———. *No Boundary: Eastern and Western Approaches to Personal Growth*. Boulder: Shambhala, 1981.

———. *Spectrum of Consciousness*. Wheaton, Ill.: The Theosophical Publishing House, 1977.

———. *Up from Eden: A Transpersonal View of Human Evolution*. Garden City: Doubleday, Anchor Press, 1981.

Woodman, Marion. *Addiction to Perfection*. Toronto: Inner City Books, 1982.

———. *The Owl Was a Baker's Daughter*. Toronto: Inner City Books, 1980.

———. *The Pregnant Virgin*. Toronto: Inner City Books, 1985.

———. *The Ravaged Bridegroom*. Toronto: Inner City Books, 1990.

Index

Other titles for your personal and spiritual journey . . .

Growing Whole: Exploring the Wilderness Within
An Audio and Guided Journal for Discovering Your Strengths, Creativity, and Wisdom
by Molly Young Brown

Explore the amazing possibilities you possess with this unique "mini-seminar." It combines an audio tape and a journal to provide you with guided meditation, inner dialogue, writing, and drawing exercises. These exercises help you recognize your strengths and discover how your inner resources—wisdom, love, and creativity—can improve your life and the lives of those around you. 60-min. audio, 128 pp. journal.
Order No. 8329

The Kitchen Mystic
Spiritual Lessons Hidden in Everyday Life
by Mary Hayes-Grieco

With humor and grace, *The Kitchen Mystic* combines everyday tasks with the spiritual quest. Blending ideas and insights from the Twelve Steps, religious principles, and spiritual philosophies, these short essays explore topics such as the marvels of an onion's layers, the lessons your children offer, and the ripple effects of neighborhood cleanups. This book taps into life's mysteries in a way guaranteed to lighten your heart. 110 pp.
Order No. 5069

Green Spirituality
Reflections on Belonging to a World Beyond Myself
by Veronica Ray

To help answer the question, "What am I becoming spiritual for?" the author provides meditations about moving beyond personal growth. A deepening spirituality, she suggests, brings you a sense of caring for the human family. Themes to reflect on include "My Self," "Myself and Others," "Myself and My Communities," and "Myself and the Earth." This inspirational book helps you to become more spiritually aware. 128 pp.
Order No. 5184
